Cataloging Correctly for Kids

An Introduction to the Tools

FOURTH EDITION

EDITED BY

Sheila S. Intner

Joanna F. Fountain

Jane E. Gilchrist

Association for Library Collections and Technical Services

American Library Association
Chicago   2006

Composition by ALA Editions in Friz Quadrata and Minion using QuarkXPress 5.0 on a PC platform.

Printed on 50-pound white offset, a pH-neutral stock, and bound in 10-point coated cover stock by Victor Graphics.

The paper used in this publication meets the minimum requirements of American National Standard for Information Sciences—Permanence of Paper for Printed Library Materials, ANSI Z39.48-1992. ⊗

Library of Congress Cataloging-in-Publication Data

Cataloging correctly for kids : an introduction to the tools / edited by Sheila S. Intner, Joanna F. Fountain and Jane E. Gilchrist.— 4th ed.
      p.   cm.
    Includes bibliographical references and index.
    ISBN 0-8389-3559-1 (alk. paper)
    1. Cataloging of children's literature—United States. I. Intner, Sheila S.
  II. Fountain, Joanna F. III. Gilchrist, Jane E.
    Z695.1.C6C37 2005
    025.3'2—dc22   2005018838

Printed in the United States of America

10   09   08   07   06   5   4   3   2   1

Contents

Introduction

Sheila S. Intner

Everywhere librarians turn these days, they are urged to attend closely to the needs of the people they serve. "Customer service" has become a byword of the profession. At the same time, and, for that matter, in the service of this very ideal, librarians are working hard to combine their efforts to meet the greatly increased expectations of today's library patrons about what materials should be available and how those materials can be obtained. As a result, it is more difficult than ever for catalog librarians to tread the fine line between customizing services for local users and conforming to uniform service standards for the widest possible community of patrons, many of whom are located far from the local library's jurisdiction. This book aims to help librarians whose main focus is the library's youngest customers—kids—find the best way to provide cataloging and classification services suited to the special needs of this group while faithfully meeting the standards on which the rest of the community depends.

Cataloging and classification services are basic to the provision of all materials to every person who uses libraries as well as to the provision of reference services based on the materials held in library collections. The catalog is the principal tool used by every person, regardless of age, who wants to find materials in a library. It is the only tool for people of all ages who are not able to go to the library, but can reach it through the online catalog. A good catalog should provide excellent service to all who use it—again, regardless of age. Yet, before the first publication of *Cataloging Correctly for Kids* in 1989, little guidance was available in how cataloging and classification standards designed with adult materials in mind might be applied equally well to materials intended for kids. (A notable exception to this absence of guidance came from the Library of Congress, which began its Annotated Card [AC] program decades earlier.)

For sixteen years *Cataloging Correctly for Kids* has filled the gap. In addition to chapters that explained in clear language each of the standards, rules, and tools they needed to apply, catalogers working with kids' materials have had an essential document to guide them in preparing records that were both appropriate and standardized: "Guidelines for Standardized Cataloging of Children's Materials." Subsequent editions in 1991 and 1998 have kept the Guidelines current, along with the information covering various rules and tools. This edition continues the tradition of updating the Guidelines, which follow this introduction in chapter 1.

The Guidelines are an important contribution of the Cataloging and Classification Section of the Association for Library Collections and Technical Services. Although the principal work has been done by the Section's Cataloging of Children's Materials Committee, which is responsible for all editions of *Cataloging Correctly for Kids*, other committees were also involved, including the Committee on Cataloging: Description and Access, the Subject Analysis Committee, and the Executive Committee of the Association itself, which voted to approve it in each of its iterations. A good many more committees and groups are represented by liaisons to the Cataloging of Children's Materials Committee. Their participation helped ensure that the advice offered by this book is cognizant of and sensitive to the concerns of many different constituencies and that it addresses those concerns to the greatest extent possible.

Following the Guidelines the text continues with an assessment, underlying all the methodological detail, of "How Children Search," by Lynne A. Jacobsen. Meeting the needs of searchers is the aim of all cataloging and should be the foundation on which we build catalog records. Deborah A. Fritz goes on to explain how two of our most important cataloging standards function in "Cataloging Correctly Using AACR2 and MARC 21," and follows this with a chapter titled "Copy Cataloging Correctly," which covers appropriate methods of using cataloging from sources outside the local library in preparing its catalog.

In chapter 5, "Authority Control," Kay E. Lowell describes how to create and maintain a catalog using standard heading forms. Joanna F. Fountain continues exploring subject headings in the following chapter, "Using LC's Children's Headings for Original MARC Cataloging: Why and How." Joseph Miller continues discussing subject heading authorities in "Sears List of Subject Headings," and Gregory R. New goes on to examine classification authorities in "Sources for Dewey Numbers."

Sheila S. Intner covers the special concerns about materials other than books in chapter 9, "Cataloging Nonbook Materials," making a strong case for extending standard treatments to all library materials, regardless of their physical forms. Joanna F. Fountain then follows with a chapter describing "How the CIP Program Helps Children's Librarians."

School and public libraries are the most obvious places that focus on collecting materials for kids, but they are not the only ones. Gabriele I. Kupitz explains the role of children's materials in college and university libraries in the first part of a chapter titled "Cataloging for Kids in the Academic Library." In the second part of the chapter, Vickie Frierson-Adams reports revealing statistics about such collections, gathered in a study conducted recently.

The two chapters that follow discuss important management issues: "Automating the Children's Catalog," by Pamela J. Newberg and Judith Yurczyk, and "Vendors of Cataloging for Children's Materials," by Newberg and Jennifer Allen. An excellent bibliography of sources, prepared by Virginia M. Overberg and Brigid Burke, helps you continue adding to your knowledge of good cataloging. Finally, brief biographical sketches for each author can be found in the final pages of the book.

As principal editor, I gratefully acknowledge the work, advice, contributions, and encouragement of each person who participated in the preparation of this edition of *Cataloging Correctly for Kids*. There are many more than I can name here. Any errors of omission or commission, however, are mine and should not be attributed to the experts who wrote, read, and commented on the Guidelines or parts of the text or both, or to my colleagues Joanna Fountain and Jane E. Gilchrist, who shared the job of editing the text.

Individuals who merit very special mention include Joanna Fountain and Jane Gilchrist, Library of Congress, my coeditors; Sara Shatford Layne, president of the Association for Library Collections and Technical Services; Oksana Kraus, chair of the Association's Cataloging and Classification Section and chair of the Cataloging of Children's Materials Committee; and Charles Wilt, executive director of the association, all of whom helped turn this project into a reality. *Cataloging Correctly for Kids*, fourth edition, is the result of a happy collaboration among us all—editors, authors, members of the Cataloging of Children's Materials Committee, and leaders of the section and the association. We earnestly hope it aids you in your pursuit of better library service to kids.

1

Guidelines for Standardized Cataloging for Children

Joanna F. Fountain, for the Association for Library Collections and Technical Services, Cataloging and Classification Section, Cataloging of Children's Materials Committee

The library community has long recognized that children have their own unique characteristics and requirements as library users. They are considered a different enough audience, as users of both print and nonprint materials, that special bibliographic treatment of library materials is warranted to meet their developmental needs. Many adult users of libraries—especially parents, teachers, and other caregivers—will also benefit from this treatment when they are using catalogs created to provide simple and full information about the content of library materials for younger and less sophisticated readers.

Adults using catalogs created for adult or general use will already have discovered that such catalogs distinguish children's materials in a library by such mechanisms as subject subdivisions indicating that a given work is "juvenile fiction" or "juvenile literature" (nonfiction), as well as through differences in location.

Background

In recognition of the unique nature of juvenile library users and in response to their needs, the Library of Congress (LC) established the Annotated Card (AC) program in 1966. Currently administered by the Children's Literature Team, History and Literature Cataloging Division, the program has adapted the Library's cataloging policies and practices to include annotations, modified subject heading usage, and some special classification options. The AC program was originally accessed through catalog cards from the Library of Congress and is now available through MARC (Machine-Readable Cataloging) records and LC's Cataloging-in-Publication (CIP) program.

1

During the 1960s, as libraries found it cheaper or more convenient to rely on commercial or centralized processing services, it became apparent that standardization of cataloging practices was necessary. More recently, many libraries began contributing records to shared databases, lending further weight to the need for standardization. A study by the Cataloging of Children's Materials Committee of the Resources and Technical Services Division (RTSD) of the American Library Association (ALA) found that the lack of a uniform standard meant that many libraries developed customized cataloging according to their own perceived needs or accepted nonstandard cataloging from other sources.

The cost of customized cataloging, however, cuts into other services, and if the source of cataloging changes, so do the style and standard of cataloging. The Cataloging of Children's Materials Committee also foresaw that the development of MARC standards and widely used bibliographic utilities offered potential for the wider dissemination of standardized cataloging if guidelines for standardization could be developed and followed. In response, the Committee recommended in 1969 that LC's practices for cataloging children's materials be adopted as a national standard. This recommendation was subsequently adopted by the Cataloging and Classification Section of RTSD. (RTSD was renamed the Association for Library Collections and Technical Services in 1989 and is now known by the acronym ALCTS.)

Since the original Guidelines were developed, many more libraries have benefited from shared cataloging efforts, either through bibliographic utilities or commercial processors using MARC records, so that it is now even more advantageous in terms of cost and data compatibility to accept this standardization. The creation and exchange of bibliographic data at an international level, and access to these data by commercial processors as well as by libraries, have led the ALA to accept LC's cataloging for children's materials as a standard. In 1982, the Cataloging of Children's Materials Committee, with the cooperation of the Children's Literature Section (more recently renamed the Children's Literature Team, History and Literature Cataloging Division) at LC, developed the "Guidelines for Standardized Cataloging of Children's Materials," which were accepted by the RTSD Board of Directors on July 14, 1982.

Widespread use of MARC records has made it possible for many smaller libraries to automate their catalogs, converting retrospectively from card catalogs to online and World Wide Web (Web) catalogs, and acquiring current machine-readable records from LC, materials vendors, and specialized vendors of cataloging data for use in online computer systems. International developments in content and MARC standards in turn suggest the need for again updating the Guidelines for policies and practices for cataloging library materials for children, which were last revised in 1996.

Scope

The Guidelines are intended for use in cataloging all materials deemed intellectually suitable for children and young people. Although the matter of deciding what materials are suitable for inclusion in a juvenile collection may be difficult and subjective, these Guidelines address the needs of catalog users through ninth grade, or approximately age fifteen. Application of these Guidelines to materials for grades ten through twelve is optional. LC considers materials to be "juvenile" works when they are intended by the author or publisher, or deemed suitable by the cataloger, for use by children and young people in these age and grade ranges. Catalogers in libraries with juvenile collections are encouraged to consider implementing the LC standard to all PreK–12, or ages newborn through eighteen, if their collections include materials for teens at all levels.

Agencies that contribute cataloging to a shared database using the MARC format place an appropriate code in the fixed-field character position for target audience (Books field 008 position 22), indicating the intended level of the material. Code j indicates that the item is intended for general use by children and young people through the age of fifteen or the ninth grade. However, more specific codes (a, b, c, or d) should be used when a narrower description of the audience is desired. If an item is appropriate for more than one audience, the code for the principal target audience is assigned. The audience codes are defined as follows:

a   Preschool (up to, but not including, kindergarten)

b   Primary (kindergarten through grade 3)

c   Preadolescent (grades 4 through 8)

d   Adolescent (grades 9 through 12)

g   General (any audience level)

j   Juvenile (all through age fifteen or grade 9)

These Guidelines are compatible with national cataloging tools and should be used in conjunction with them. Currently these tools include:

Anglo-American Cataloguing Rules, 2nd edition (AACR2) with its latest revision and amendments;

Library of Congress Rule Interpretations (LCRI)—LC policies and interpretations of AACR2;

Cataloger's Desktop—a CD-ROM and Web subscription product that includes the most-used cataloging documentation resources in electronic form;

Library of Congress Subject Headings (LCSH), including AC modifications and principles for applying them, as issued annually and published daily on the Web at http://authorities.loc.gov when these differ from instructions published in *Subject Cataloging Manual: Subject Headings*, which are intended for application of subject headings in nonjuvenile catalogs; and

Abridged Dewey Decimal Classification and Relative Index (14th or most current edition), or *Library of Congress Classification* schedules.

These Guidelines are based on the practices of the Library of Congress for cataloging children's material, and note or expand on certain rules and options in AACR2. Rules, options, and practices that are not touched on are not meant to be excluded. References within this text to individual rules are to rules in the current edition of AACR2. Although some MARC 21 field numbers and subfield codes are identified in the Guidelines, complete instructions and further information about MARC 21 may be found online at http://www.loc.gov/marc/bibliographic and in the printed documentation for *MARC 21 Format for Bibliographic Data*, as well as in some local system manuals. Some commonly used MARC 21 fields are listed in figure 1-1.

Figure 1-1.   MARC 21 Bibliographic Fields Commonly Used in Juvenile Records

010	Library of Congress Control Number (LCCN)
020	International Standard Book Number (ISBN)
050	Library of Congress Call Number
082	Dewey Decimal Classification
100	Main entry—Personal name
110	Main entry—Corporate name
130	Main entry—Uniform title
245	Title statement
246	Varying form of title
250	Edition statement
260	Publication, distribution, etc. (Imprint)
300	Physical description
440	Series statement/Added entry—Title
490	Series statement

500	General note
505	Formatted contents note
508	Creation/Production credits note
511	Participant or performer note
520	Summary note
521	Target audience note
526	Study program information note
538	System details note
546	Language note
586	Awards note
600	Subject added entry—Personal name
650	Subject added entry—Topical term
651	Subject added entry—Geographic name
655	Index term—Genre/Form term
658	Index term—Curriculum objective
700	Added entry—Personal name
710	Added entry—Corporate name
730	Added entry—Uniform title
800	Series added entry—Personal name
830	Series added entry—Uniform title
856	Electronic location and access

Guidelines for Description and Access

These Guidelines address the following:

> Description of print and nonprint—including electronic—materials and resources
>
> Name, title, and series access points for various types of materials
>
> Subject heading use for juvenile catalogs
>
> Classification of juvenile collections

Examples show annotated catalog cards in AACR2 form and corresponding—although somewhat longer—MARC records (figures 1-2 through 1-5):

Figure 1-2.   Example of an Annotated Catalog Card for a Book

---

Fic   Kadohata, Cynthia.
        Kira-kira / Cynthia Kadohata. — 1st ed. — New York : Atheneum Books
for Young Readers, c2004.
        244 p. ; 19 cm.
        Summary: Chronicles the close friendship between two Japanese-
American sisters growing up in rural Georgia during the late 1950s and early
1960s, and the despair when one sister becomes terminally ill.
        ISBN 0-689-85639-6
        1. [Sisters—Fiction. 2. Friendship—Fiction. 3. Japanese Americans—
Fiction. 4. Death—Fiction. 5. Georgia—History—20th century—Fiction.]
I. Title.
        PZ7.K1166 Ki 2004   [Fic]—dc22   2003000737

Figure 1-3.   Example of a MARC 21 Record for a Book

Leader   01495cam 2200325 a 450
005   20041228210354.0
008   030122s2004 nyu c 000 1 eng
010 __ |a   2003000737
020 __ |a 0689856393
040 __ |a DLC |c DLC |d DLC |d TxGeoBT
042 __ |a lcac
050 00 |a PZ7.K1166 |b Ki 2004
082 00 |a [Fic] |2 22
100 1 |a Kadohata, Cynthia.
245 10 |a Kira-kira / |c Cynthia Kadohata
250 |a 1st ed.
260 |a New York : |b Atheneum Books for Young Readers, |c c2004.
300 |a 244 p. ; |c 19 cm.
520 |a Chronicles the close friendship between two Japanese-American sisters
         growing up in rural Georgia during the late 1950s and early 1960s, and the
         despair when one sister becomes terminally ill.
586 |a Newbery Award, 2004
650 1 |a Sisters |v Fiction.
650 1 |a Friendship |v Fiction.
650 1 |a Japanese Americans |v Fiction.
650 1 |a Death |v Fiction.
651 1 |a Georgia |x History |y 20th century |v Fiction.
856 42 |3 Contributor biographical information:
         |u http://www.loc.gov/catdir/bios/simon053/2003000737.html
856 42 |3 Publisher description:
         |u http://www.loc.gov/catdir/description/simon052/2003000737.html

Figure 1-4.   Example of an Annotated Catalog Card for a Nonbook Item

031   Microsoft Encarta 2004 encyclopedia deluxe [electronic resource]. —
            Redmond, WA : Microsoft Corp., c2003.
            3 computer optical discs : sd., col. ; 4 3/4 in.
System requirements: Multimedia PC with 300MB available hard-disk space and
4MB of video memory; CD-ROM drive. Some features require an Internet
connection and current browser.
            Title from CD-ROM disc label.
            Summary: A computerized encyclopedia that includes feature articles,
photographs, illustrations, videos, animations, sound and music clips, map
locations, 3-D virtual tours, an English dictionary and translation dictionaries
for text, videos and audio.
1. Electronic encyclopedias. I. Microsoft Corporation. II. Title: Encarta
2004 encyclopedia deluxe
 	
.AE5   031—dc22   2003692556

Figure 1-5.   Example of a MARC 21 Record for a Nonbook Item

Leader 01704cmm 22002895a 4500
    005 20040205143812.0
    007 co |||||||||||
    008 031124s2003 wau m eng
    010 __ |a 2003692556
    040 __ |a EHI |c EHI |d DLC |d TxGeoBT
    042 __ |a lccopycat
    050 00 |a AE5
    082 14 |a 031 |2 14
    245 00 |a Microsoft Encarta 2004 encyclopedia deluxe |h [electronic resource]
    246 30 |a Encarta 2004 encyclopedia deluxe
            |h [electronic resource]
    260 __ |a Redmond, WA : |b Microsoft Corp., |c c2003.
    300 __ |a 3 computer optical discs : |b sd., col. ; |c 4 3/4 in.
    538 __ |a A computerized encyclopedia that includes feature articles, photographs,
            illustrations, videos, animations, sound and music clips, map locations, 3-D
            virtual tours, an English dictionary and translation dictionaries for text,
            videos and audio.
    500 __ |a Title from CD-ROM disc label.
    650 _1 |a Electronic encyclopedias.
    710 2_ |a Microsoft Corporation.

Description

The description of the material to be cataloged must follow the second or third level of description as found in Rule 1.0D2 in AACR2. Although many libraries have previously used abbreviated cataloging similar to the first level of description, the first level of description does not provide for elements that are considered important by many libraries and, therefore, are required by the Guidelines. These elements include statements of responsibility (including subsequent statements of responsibility such as "illustrated by . . ."), dimensions, and series information. Elements that require clarification or for which specific treatment is suggested are discussed more fully in the following sections.

GMD

The GMD, or general material designation (Rule 1.1C) (subfield h of MARC field 245), is optional in AACR2 and selectively applied in LCRI, but is strongly recommended in these Guidelines for *all* formats of materials in List 2 (other than the rarely used GMD "text"). The GMD should appear in square brackets immediately following the title proper, because its purpose is to identify the broad class of material to which an item belongs and to distinguish between different forms of the same work at an early stage in the description. It precedes any other title information, such as a subtitle. Use of the GMD text is optional. Most agencies do not use it for books, because library users normally assume that the record describes a book.

Notes

AACR2 provides for many optional elements. The note area of the catalog record has probably the widest range of options. Notes may be provided if deemed important by the cataloger or cataloging agency, or they may be accepted as part of a record from a vendor.

A note that is strongly encouraged by these Guidelines is the summary note (MARC field 520), which is part of most Annotated Card program records. It consists of an objective statement of the most important elements of the plot, theme, or topic of the work. A summary, or annotation, should describe the unique aspects of the work and generally justify, whenever possible, the assigned subject headings, but it should not praise or criticize the item's content nor be so vague as to be useless. Words in the summary should be chosen to facilitate keyword searching in online catalogs, using synonyms for words found in the title and subject headings, for example. Users of nonbook items are especially dependent on summary notes because of the greater difficulty of browsing such materials. However, a summary note is not required if a contents note (MARC field 505) that is descriptive of the nature and the scope of the work is used. A contents note is used to record the titles of individual selections contained in an item such as a book, sound recording, or videorecording. AACR2 specifies the order in which notes are to be given. If both the summary note (MARC 520) and the contents note (MARC 505) are present, the contents note will often be the last note in the record.

Information about system requirements (MARC field 538, System details note) should be provided for videorecordings, electronic resources, and some sound recordings.

The participant or performer note (MARC field 511) is used to list names of performers or cast members on sound recordings and videorecordings.

Two other notes are especially applicable to juvenile materials. Target audience notes (MARC field 521) contain information about reading grade level, interest age level, or interest grade level of the intended audience of an item. Because more than one may be provided, the source of the statement of level must always be included, as measures and opinions often do not agree. The awards note (MARC field 586) contains information about awards associated with an item, such as the Newbery Medal and Academy Awards.

ISBN

The International Standard Book Number (ISBN) (MARC field 020) is required when available. The area for standard number and terms of availability (price) follows the area for notes on cards. In a MARC record, the ISBN is given near the beginning of the record, before the rest of the description.

Name, Title, and Series Access Points

There is no variation from AACR2 in either choice or form of main entry for children's materials. The form of added entries for names and titles also remains the same. (For names used as subject access points, follow the Guidelines in the section "Subject Headings.") The choice of added entries for names and titles and the choice and form of series added entries are discussed here.

Name Access Points

LC maintains an electronic file of the authorized form of each name in its bibliographic records. The authorized form is established according to the rules in part 2 of AACR2, along with various rule interpretations (LCRIs) and options that appear there. LC staff also train other librarians to apply these rules and interpretations and to create MARC authority records for each type of name—personal, corporate, geographic, event—and titles (series and uniform titles) as part of the name authority component (NACO) of the Program for Cooperative Cataloging. Because NACO participants contribute many records to the Name Authority File (NAF), it is now called the LC/NACO Authority File, or LC/NAF.

Currently, about six million authority records exist. Of this total, names, series titles, uniform titles, and name/title combinations are found in the LC/NAF, while topical subjects—including the names of fictitious characters—are found in the LC/SACO Subject Authority File (see the section "Subject Headings"). LC and NACO participants add thousands of records each year, and all are freely available for consultation, copying/pasting, and downloading at http://www.loc.gov/catdir/pcc/naco.html. Librarians developing catalogs for young and less sophisticated readers should always verify and use the form of names and titles in the LC/NAF (or the LC/SACO Subject Authority File) so searchers are not confused by multiple forms for the same person or body.

In bibliographic records, added entries for individuals (MARC field 700) and groups or corporate bodies (MARC field 710) are provided to improve access to names in bibliographic records other than those names used as main entries, which are usually only the primary or first-named author of a work.

1. Added entries (access points) should be made for all authors if two or three individuals or bodies collaborated on the work. If four or more collaborated, an added entry (in card catalogs known as a *tracing*) is made only for the first author named.
2. Added entries for illustrators are required, as their contribution to a work may equal or overshadow that of a writer. Access to the record by illustrators' names is important not only for the artistic content but also for collocating works of artists. If the illustrator is also the author of the work, a separate added entry is not made. For illustrators whose contribution consists only of the cover, frontispiece, or incidental or repeating chapter-head decorations, or for designers who are not also the illustrators, added entries are optional.
3. Added entries should be made for principal performers on sound recordings, and for producers, directors, and writers of videorecordings unless there are more than three of each. If there are four or more, make an added entry only under the one named first in each category.
4. Although AACR2 allows the optional use of function designations for editors, compilers, and the like (subfield e of MARC field 700), only the designation ill. (for *illustrator*) is required by these Guidelines.

Title Access Points

Use the following rules from AACR2 in making added title entries:

1. Make an added entry for the title even if the title proper (MARC field 245, subfield a) is the same as an assigned subject heading. Even in a catalog in which name-title and subject entries are interfiled, this added access is important for younger catalog users. It is also essential for divided card catalogs and online catalogs, as the title must appear as an entry in the title index itself, thus allowing for retrieval by title alone.
2. Make an added entry for the title even if the title proper is the same as the main entry heading for a personal or corporate name.

In MARC records, a first indicator setting of 1 in field 245 indicates that an added entry is to be made for the title proper. Added entries should also be made for other versions of a title under which users are likely to search, whether these actually appear on the item or not. Varying forms of titles are recorded in MARC field 246 with the first indicator set to 1 or 3 so these titles will be indexed and retrievable in a title search. The authorized forms of many names (personal, corporate, etc.) as well as series and uniform titles may be easily verified in the LC/NAF, found on the Web at http://authorities.loc.gov.

Series Access Points

Series access is particularly important for children's materials because the series is a source of information about the content and approach of a work.

Make a series added entry for each work in the series that is cataloged if it provides a useful access point. Add the number of the individual work within the series if there is a number. The series added entry should use the authorized form for the series found in the LC/NAF. If the authorized form of the series appears on the item, it is recorded in field 440 of the MARC record, for example,

> 440 _0 |a Girltalk ; |v no. 10

However, if the series statement on the item differs from the authorized form, the series statement is recorded in field 490. The first indicator in the 490 field specifies whether there will be an added series entry and whether it will be indexed. A first indicator of 0 specifies that the series title will not be indexed, and a setting of 1 specifies that the series will be indexed but that the authorized form of the entry will be found in a subsequent 8XX field. For example, when the authorized form of the series has a personal name as the first element, it is entered in an 800 field:

> 490 1 |a Alphabet books
>
> 800 1 |a Moncure, Jane Belk. |t Alphabet books

Series added entries may be uniform titles, such as:

     800 1_   Shakespeare, William, |d 1564-1616. |t Works. |f 1999 ; |v v. 6

When the title is the first element in the authorized form of the series, it is entered in field 830:

     490 1 |a Kids make a difference

     830 _0 |a Reading expeditions series. |p Kids make a difference

    Authorized forms of many series titles are freely available on LC's website at http://authorities.loc.gov. Each title should be checked against that file to ensure accuracy and to prevent confusion in the catalog.

Subject Headings

Until the Library of Congress's Subject Authority File was made available on the Web, the best print source for subject headings was the most recent edition of the *Library of Congress Subject Headings* (LCSH) and its list of Annotated Card (AC) program headings. The online version, which contains records contributed by participants in the Subject Authority Cooperative program, is called the LC/SACO Subject Authority File (LC/SAF). It is somewhat more current, but because AC terms are rarely changed and the printed version includes the AC usage guidelines—including subdivision practice—in addition to the list, the print edition is still invaluable. The list contains terms created as alternatives to terms in the main list to offer more appropriate subject headings for juvenile catalog users and to afford them easier subject access to materials.

    Any heading chosen from a printed copy of LCSH should be checked against the list of AC headings or online to see if there is an AC exception to it. The list of AC headings appears in the front of the first volume of the printed edition and in two web versions—Classification Web and Library of Congress Authorities. Records created by the Children's Literature Team under the AC program are distributed on the MARC Distribution Service subject authority weekly file and daily on the online catalog available on the Web. AC records may be identified by a value of b in MARC field 008 position 11. Subject headings—both LC main and AC—used on records for juvenile materials created by LC staff are also listed in *Subject Headings for Children* (OCLC, 1993 or later) and in *Subject Headings for School and Public Libraries* (Libraries Unlimited, 2001 or later).

    Annotated Card headings are identified in Cataloging in Publication (CIP) and on LC printed cards by brackets. Record and card printing programs may be programmed to delete or keep the bracketed information, as required by the individual library. In MARC bibliographic records, a second indicator setting of 1 in MARC 6XX fields identifies AC headings or usage. Subject headings may also be added from the *Sears List of Subject Headings*, either by a vendor or local cataloging agency, with the second indicator set to 7 and the code "sears" provided in subfield 2 to identify the source of the term. If the cataloger is using OCLC (Online Computer Library Center) standards, the second indicator in the 6XX field should be set to 8 for Sears subject headings.

Application of AC Subject Headings and Subdivisions

Some AC headings are simplified forms of standard LC headings, but the chief differences between AC and LC headings are in the AC rules for application of subject headings. Review the full details, found in the front matter in LCSH volume 1; only a brief summary is provided here:

1. Omission of the subdivision —**Juvenile literature** and related subdivisions such as —**Juvenile films** and —**Juvenile fiction.**
2. Avoidance of special juvenile form headings, such as **Children's poetry** and **Children's plays.**
3. Avoidance of the term **American** and the subdivision —**United States** when the subject is universal in nature. Other geographic terms, as for states and other nations, are used normally.
4. Deletion of words in topical headings that would be superfluous in a juvenile catalog. For example, **Parties** is used instead of **Children's parties.**
5. Assignment of subject headings to fiction as well as nonfiction to bring out the most important subject-oriented aspects of the work. The subdivision —**Fiction** is used when appropriate for subject headings applied to fictional material.
6. Assignment of both general and specific headings (e.g., **Turtles** and **Sea turtles**) to a work if both provide useful subject access.
7. Assignment of heading's designating form (e.g., **Jokes; Stories in rhyme**) whenever access by form of material appears helpful.
8. Assignment of both popular and scientific terms (e.g., **Cats** and **Felidae**) for the same work, depending on whether the material is intended for very young children or older children or both. Note, however, that the AC list customarily substitutes common names of animals and plants for scientific ones in the LC standard list.
9. Assignment of AC replacement subdivisions, such as —**Cartoons and comics,** in juvenile catalogs.

Creation of New Subject Headings

If the AC list and LCSH do not provide suitable terminology for the children's materials at hand, the following steps may be taken:

1. Refer to other established subject heading lists, such as *Sears List of Subject Headings*, for headings not found in LCSH.
2. Contact LC to suggest new subject headings for the AC list or LCSH at http://www.loc.gov/catdir/pcc/prop/proposal.html.
3. Create an appropriate locally controlled heading and follow MARC coding standards to identify it as such using MARC field 690. If the term will be an uncontrolled index term only, use field 653.

Use of MARC Field 658 for Curricular Objectives

If it is deemed important to list index terms denoting curriculum or course-study objectives applicable to the materials being described, use terms found in published local or state sources in subfield a and identify the source in subfield 2 of the MARC 658 field. Other subfields in this field are optional.

Classification

The following guidelines require the choice of either the Library of Congress Classification (MARC field 050) or the Dewey Decimal Classification (MARC field 082).

Library of Congress Classification

1. For fiction, assign numbers from the PZ schedule.
2. For nonfiction materials, assign numbers from the appropriate nonfiction schedule.

Dewey Decimal Classification

1. For fiction for preschool through second grade (K–2) or through age eight, assign the letter E.
2. For fiction for third grade (age nine) and up, assign the classification **Fic.** (In the first edition of these Guidelines, grade three was included in Easy collections. The policy limiting the classification E to materials for users through grade two was implemented at the Library of Congress in August 1994.)
3. For biography, any of the following practices is appropriate:

    the letter B for any individual biography;

the number 92 for individual biography and 920 for collective biography; or

the class number representing the subject of the person's most noted contribution, as instructed in the current abridged edition of the *Dewey Decimal Classification.*

4. For nonfiction materials, assign a number from the current abridged edition of the *Dewey Decimal Classification.* Options for treatment of biography are described in item 3 of this list.

Classification of Folklore

Under either Library of Congress or Dewey classification, use these Guidelines to determine whether an item is folklore:

1. Folklore is defined as those items of culture that are learned orally, by imitation or by observation, including narratives (tales, legends, proverbs, etc.). A story about fairies is not folklore unless it meets the criterion of having been handed down orally from generation to generation. It might be a modern piece of fantasy fiction instead.
2. Regard relatively faithful retellings and adaptations of folk material as folklore.
3. Do not consider religious mythology, stories from the Bible or other religious scriptures, modern fantasies, or drastic alterations of folk material as folklore, but class them elsewhere.

Local Implementation

Adopting this standard does not require libraries or catalogers to use records created by LC or to accept all elements of records available online or through commercial vendors. Data manipulation and design of local cataloging profiles are accommodated by most machine-readable formats and are provided by most commercial vendors and utilities. However, libraries that contribute to shared databases and vendors who supply MARC records are expected to conform to standards. Libraries that do not use computer services now may well do so in the future. It is thus to the advantage of all libraries to have a recommended standard for cataloging juvenile materials. As a further benefit, by making children's cataloging compatible with that for adult materials—without sacrificing its unique characteristics—this standard enables the young user to understand the adult catalog.

These Guidelines give sufficient latitude for the individual cataloger or library to meet local needs while remaining within the standard. The recommendations in these Guidelines are intended to meet the requirements of young library users, in accordance with the purpose of the catalog record.

Sources for Consultation

Abridged Dewey Decimal Classification and Relative Index. [14th or more current ed.] Dublin, OH: OCLC.

Anglo-American Cataloguing Rules. 2nd ed., 2002 rev. and updates. Chicago: American Library Association.

Fountain, Joanna F. *Subject Headings for School and Public Libraries: An LCSH/Sears Companion.* 3rd or more current ed. Westport, CT: Libraries Unlimited.

Furrie, Betty. *Understanding MARC Bibliographic: Machine-Readable Cataloging.* 7th or more current ed. Washington, DC: Library of Congress Cataloging Distribution Service.

Gorman, Michael. *The Concise AACR2.* 4th or more current ed. Chicago: American Library Association.

Library of Congress. Cataloging Policy and Support Office. *Library of Congress Classification Schedules.* Washington, DC: Library of Congress.

————. Cataloging Policy and Support Office. *Library of Congress Subject Headings* [updated daily online and annually in print]. Washington, DC: Library of Congress.

————. Cataloging Policy and Support Office. *Subject Cataloging Manual: Subject Headings* [updated online and in print as needed]. Washington, DC: Library of Congress.

————. Network Development and MARC Standards Office. *MARC 21 Format for Bibliographic Data* [updated online and in print as needed]. Washington, DC: Library of Congress.

2

How Children Search

Lynne A. Jacobsen

A clear understanding of how children search and retrieve information is critical to providing quality cataloging that will enable children to successfully
find information. Understanding how children search also impacts the design of
information retrieval systems, which provide electronic access to websites, databases, and library materials. With the proliferation of electronic information, its
ubiquitous nature, and its increased use in education, the need to understand children's searching behavior has never been greater.

Children in second grade and above are expected to find information using
electronic means. Children at this stage are just beginning to learn to read. As a
result, they tend to rely more on visual and auditory information than on textual
information. Young children (five to ten years old) are being forced to negotiate
digital library interfaces that require complex typing and proper spelling and reading skills, or that necessitate an understanding of abstract concepts or content
knowledge beyond young children's still-developing abilities.[1] They are just beginning to enter the developmental stage where they can classify objects and understand hierarchical structure, so it is difficult for children to come up with subject
headings and synonyms to use in constructing searches. Children use natural language. They are not familiar with controlled vocabulary terms, such as Sears or
Library of Congress subject headings, which require knowledge of words above the
sixth-grade reading level. They have trouble selecting the correct form of a word.
For example, the search term "Dog" will not retrieve hits if "Dogs" is the indexed
search term. As a result, children prefer browse searching.

Children navigating the Web experience the same difficulties as they do when
searching online public access catalogs. Children lack the ability to effectively scan

the inevitably large retrieval sets of information generated from searches. Because children lack a developed recall memory, they have problems modifying a search. Boolean searching and search limiters improve the precision of keyword searching, but these concepts are too complicated for children ten and under. For these reasons, children have low success when searching electronic resources. Although older children in middle school have greater knowledge bases, mechanical skills, and cognitive skills, they still may fail to locate needed information.

Solutions to the difficulties that children experience in searching may include improved interface design and enhanced cataloging practices. Spell-checkers can help children with spelling difficulties. Amazon.com gently asks users "Did you mean . . .?" when a misspelled search term is entered. A natural language processor can help children overcome the constraints of controlled vocabulary. Ask Jeeves for Kids is an example of a search engine that uses natural language processing.

Hierarchical directory structures address the problems children have with spelling and knowledge of subject terms. Graphical interfaces appeal to children's preference for visual information. SearchKids is a graphical interface for children ages five to ten that allows them to successfully find information on animals. It applies the concept of scaffolding, an educational method of presenting concepts in a hierarchy. Children select picture icons representing branches in the hierarchy. For example, to find birds that live on land and water, children click on the *Animals* icon to reveal subcategories. Next, they click on a *Birds* icon. From there, they select a *Where they live* icon, followed by the subcategory of *Land and Water*. This interface performs Boolean searching, without the children having to decide between intersection and union of terms. As a result, children are quite successful in finding desired information on animals.

A new website called the International Children's Digital Library (ICDL) provides unique access to digital books for children ages three to thirteen. Children contributed to the design of the search interface, which contains colorful icons that appeal to them. Because children select books using criteria different from those used by adults, special indexes were created to enable children to find books based on the way books make them feel, such as funny or scary stories. Kids can find books by category, geography, content, setting, or format. They can also find books by size, color, length, shape, series, illustrations, or language. Children can even choose from three formats of readers (books): the standard, the spiral, and the comic book reader. These examples of search interfaces demonstrate the progress that has been made in developing search interfaces that meet the needs of children.

Enhanced cataloging practices can also improve children's access to materials in online catalogs. Catalogers must be aware of using language that children can read and understand when assigning subject headings, writing summaries, and establishing headings. Subject headings such as the Library of Congress children's subject headings assigned by the Annotated Card program are appropriate for children. The "Guidelines for Standardized Cataloging for Children" (see chapter 1) suggest assigning both broad and specific subject headings and assigning both popular and scientific terms. Implementing these ideas will help children achieve more successful searches.

A cataloger must be attentive to a book's "aboutness." Applying headings consistently enhances retrieval. It is important to bring out topics in fiction as well as nonfiction materials. Sometimes more abstract headings, such as **Fear of the dark—Fiction,** are warranted. Catalogers should use summary notes for enhancing relevant keyword access by including natural language terms.

Children's library materials come in a variety of formats. A juvenile collection can contain the same title in the form of a book, a sound recording, a videorecording, a large-print book, a board book, and a book/cassette or book/compact disc set, to name a few. Applying the same subject headings and summaries to the same work in different formats will increase the consistency of retrieval of these items. Other important access points include uniform titles and series statements. Uniform titles should be used for stories with many versions (AACR2 25.12B). Also, uniform titles provide important links to motion pictures and television programs. Many items published for children are part of a series. Children often ask for these items, so providing access to series titles is important.

Catalogers should consider assigning foreign language subject headings to foreign language materials. Subject heading thesauri are being developed, such as Sears and *Bilindex* (LC headings) in Spanish.

When cataloging items with collective titles, it is necessary to provide access to the individual titles included in the item. Titles listed in contents notes should be indexed for keyword access. Because children prefer browse searching, titles should also be provided for browse access whenever possible. Including variant forms of titles, such as cover titles, also improves access. Titles that include punctuation, acronyms, or hyphenated words should be added and indexed in each form to help children find them. Catalogers should always ask, "How might children search for this?" and then provide the necessary access points. Finally, catalogers need to be familiar with the way the fields are indexed in their own online catalogs, as this information can help in deciding whether certain access points are necessary.

Online catalogs, the Internet and World Wide Web, and other online databases continue to evolve and incorporate elements that accommodate searching behavior. Hypertext searching and precoordinated searches using picture icons are examples of elements found in online catalogs today that help users of all ages find information. More is being done to offer easy access to complex resources. A relatively new technology called *metasearch* or *federated searching* allows users to search multiple databases with a single search, as in Google searches, directly from an online catalog. Using OpenURL and resolvers, full-text journal articles can also be accessed from an online catalog. MARC (Machine-Readable Cataloging) format continues to be the format of choice for cataloging, although XML (Extensible Markup Language) is emerging as an additional format for bibliographic records. XML is proving to be better for describing data for exchange and is widely used on the Web. XML is also being considered as the means to link editions of works based on the Functional Requirements for Bibliographic Records (FRBR), which marks a distinct change from the Paris Principles of 1961. FRBR recommends that a bibliographic record represent all versions of a work, rather than having a separate bibliographic record for each version. As new developments occur, it is hoped that researchers, catalogers, and librarians will continue to keep children in mind as important catalog users.

Note

1. A. Druin et al., "A Collaborative Digital Library for Children," *Journal of Computer Assisted Learning* 19 (2003): 239.

Recommended Reading

Andresen, Leif. "After MARC—What Then?" *Library Hi Tech* 22, no. 1 (2004): 40–51.

Anglo-American Cataloguing Rules. 2nd ed., 2002 revision and updates. Chicago: American Library Association, 2002–.

Berger, Pam, ed. "Online Library for Kids." *Information Searcher* 14, no. 1 (2003): 1, 3, 21.

Bilal, Dania. "Perspectives on Children's Navigation of the World Wide Web: Does the Type of Search Task Make a Difference?" *Online Information Review* 26, no. 2 (2002): 108–16.

Broch, Elana. "Children's Search Engines from an Information Search Process Perspective." *School Library Media Research* 3, 2000. http://www.ala.org/ala/aasl/aaslpubsandjournals/slmrb/slmrcontents/volume32000/childrens.htm.

Cooper, Linda Z. "A Case Study of Information-Seeking Behavior in 7-Year-Old Children in a Semistructured Situation." *Journal of the American Society for Information Science and Technology* 53, no. 11 (September 2002): 904–22.

Druin, A., et al. "A Collaborative Digital Library for Children." *Journal of Computer Assisted Learning* 19 (2003): 239–48.

Luther, Judy. "Trumping Google: Metasearching's Promise." *Library Journal* (October 1, 2003): 36–39.

Minkel, Walter. "So Far I've Only Found His Head." *School Library Journal* (April 2000).

Pace, Andrew K. "Dismantling Integrated Library Systems." *Library Journal* (February 1, 2004): 34–36.

Revelle, Glenda, et al. "A Visual Search Tool for Early Elementary Science Students." *Journal of Science Education and Technology* 11, no. 1 (March 2002): 49–57.

3

Cataloging Correctly Using AACR2 and MARC 21

Deborah A. Fritz

Imagine this scenario: A cart sits in front of me, piled high with children's books, videos, and sound recordings, along with some educational puzzles, games, and toys, a globe, and ten "Read" posters. All this stuff on the cart (the proper term for which is *resources* rather than *stuff*, of course) cries out to be cataloged, immediately, so it can be put to work. "We should be out there satisfying the informational, educational, and/or recreational needs of our pint-sized library patrons. Please get us cataloged and out on those library shelves!"

But I'm a children's librarian, not a cataloger. I used to make up brief records for the stuff I collected for my kids. I'd file them in my little-used card catalog and get those resources out on the shelves quick-time. Then I'd get on with my real job—don't even begin to ask about all the different things I do in my workday.

Now, however, those days are gone. Although my collection is small, it has become way too big for my kids to browse the shelves to find what they want, even with my help. And I find my magic doesn't work so well anymore—staring at the ceiling and recalling, "Oh yes, I received just the right video you want last month. . . . It was in a bright blue box and I put it over . . . there."

These days I have to use my catalog to figure out what's in my collection and where I put it. It's looking more and more like past shortcuts and quickie cataloging weren't such good ideas. An author and title, a call number, and a few kid-friendly subject headings aren't proving at all useful these days. My kids want summaries. They do so much keyword searching it would really help if I had more contents notes. They want to find all our videos in Spanish, or books with illustrations of lions. They want to find individual songs on the CDs, for crying out loud! Where do they learn about all of this? They must be going to the library down the road or to other catalogs on the Web, and now they want my catalog to work the same way.

As if that weren't enough, I just found out I'm going to be putting my catalog in with the catalogs of some other libraries in something called a union catalog. It seems that making up brief entries for my records isn't going to work well in the union catalog—apparently my records do not "play well" with those from other libraries. If I don't get my information into a form that will fit in the union catalog, I can't add my records. I'll still be able to borrow from other libraries, because that's the library ethos—sharing—but I won't be able to share in return. That wouldn't be right.

I have to start following rules for cataloging my resources—something called AACR. Not only that, but I must also learn how to put the information into computer-friendly form using a standard called MARC. I became a children's librarian to work with children—I'm not a cataloger and I don't want to be one. I don't remember taking a course about cataloging at library school. What am I going to do?

Does this sound familiar? If so, you are not alone. Anyone faced with doing or overseeing the cataloging of children's materials is in the same boat with you. The good news is that help is on the way.

Cataloging Strategies

Copying someone else's cataloging is one source of help. Outsourcing your cataloging to someone else (a book jobber, publisher, cataloging service, anyone but you!) is another. More details about these kinds of assistance are in other chapters of this book. However, no one is perfect, not even the highly trained catalogers at the Library of Congress. So, whether you copy or buy records from elsewhere, you still have to know enough about AACR2 and MARC 21 to recognize problems when they occur.

With all this in mind, this chapter will introduce you to AACR2 and MARC 21, as gently as possible, and show you how important it is for you to find out how to use them both. Then you, too, can provide your kids (and maybe that union catalog) with the cataloging they need these days. First, here's a bit of a history lesson. I'll keep it short.

Cataloging Rules

The cataloging community has been developing and refining rules for a long time to standardize the way we provide bibliographic information. For now, just wrap your brain around the fact that for copy cataloging, outsourcing, and all those other methods of making cataloging faster, easier, cheaper, and better, all catalogers must (as far as humanly possible) provide the same bibliographic information whenever they describe the same resources. Try doing that without written rules! The current internationally accepted cataloging rules developed by representatives from the United States, Great Britain, Canada, and Australia, and used by most libraries in those and many other countries, are called the *Anglo-American Cataloguing Rules*, or AACR.[1]

The first edition of AACR, called AACR1, was published in 1967. A new edition, called AACR2, came out in 1978. Since then, there have been no new editions, only revisions—one in 1988 and another in 2002. In 2002, AACR changed to a loose-leaf format scheduled to be amended every summer. Replacement pages update the printed version. The digital version (on CD or the Web) is updated automatically with the purchase of a subscription. A new, third edition is currently in development. Now, that's enough cataloging history. For the grisly details, take a look at "A Brief History of AACR," an online document produced by the Joint Steering Committee for Revision of Anglo-American Cataloguing Rules, the international committee responsible for AACR.[2]

The current version of AACR has two parts. Part 1 tells us how to describe the materials we collect. It is closely based on, but not exactly the same as, another set of cataloging rules called the International Standard Bibliographic Description (ISBD).[3]

Part 2 of AACR2 tells us how to add searchable terms to the descriptions. These terms should be the ones a patron might search in an attempt to find the resources. We call the terms *access points*, *headings*, *tracings*, and other names you may encounter as you read various manuals. (We seem to like having at least two or three names for everything we talk about in cataloging.) AACR2 does not tell us how to assign subject headings or call numbers. For those instructions we must turn to controlled vocabularies and classification schemes, respectively, described elsewhere in this book.[4]

For a long time, student catalogers were taught the current versions of cataloging rules and how to enter the resulting bibliographic information on three-by-five-inch catalog cards. The cards were then meticulously filed in long, narrow catalog drawers according to yet another set of instructions (the *ALA Filing Rules*). Assuming the cards were correctly filed, patrons could search the card catalog to find the bibliographic information. Using that information, they could decide whether they wanted to take the next step of finding the materials. Lots of steps were involved, but the system worked—as long as scrupulous care was taken with every step along the way. (This scrupulous care gave catalogers a bad reputation as being persnickety and far too attached to their silly cataloging rules. But, read on—vindication is coming.)

Remember, if everyone follows the same rules to provide the same biblio-graphic information when describing the same resources, then, when one cataloger provides the bibliographic information, other catalogers can copy the information instead of having to create it all, from scratch. I ask you, where would we be these days without copy cataloging?

Copy Cataloging and the Rise of MARC

Over the years, the cataloging community tried many methods of copying cata-loging information. Some were more successful than others, but all were expensive and by no means simple. Then the Library of Congress (LC) got involved. The clever catalogers at LC began producing card sets for the materials they cataloged and began selling them at modest cost to other libraries. Any library that could afford these card sets jumped at the chance to speed up its cataloging process, and LC was soon inundated with requests for its printed cards.

More time passed, and computers came along. We progressed from writing our cards by hand to using manual and, eventually, electric typewriters, but in the late 1960s, a group of cutting-edge librarians at LC and sixteen other libraries devised a way to use the new computer technology (it was barely out of infancy) to cut down on the drudgery of producing catalog cards. They took the cataloging rules and designed a set of computer codes around them, and called the codes MARC (MAchine-Readable Cataloging). Catalogers could use these codes to enter their bibliographic information into computers instead of onto cards. Computers could then print catalog cards or produce book or microform catalogs (fiche or film), and even spine labels, book cards, and other useful by-products. Better yet, once the standards caught on, library vendors began to design circulation systems and com-puter catalogs (sometimes called OPACs, meaning Online Public Access Catalogs, and, later, WebPacs, for Web Public Access Catalogs) around the coding standards, eliminating the need to file catalog cards forever.

Before long, we discovered we could share computer records far more easily than we had been able to share cards. To facilitate this record sharing process, groups of libraries began putting records from LC with the records they made themselves into union catalogs, such as OCLC, RLIN (Research Libraries Infor-mation Network), and Utlas (University of Toronto Libraries Automated System). Libraries could then copy the records as long as they allowed everyone else to copy their records in return.

Along the way, someone thought it would be a good idea to add an identifying code to any records we made or copied. This was done, and, suddenly, it became easy to tell what libraries had which records (and therefore the materials they represented) in their collections. Once we could tell who had which resources, it became a snap to share those resources via interlibrary loan (ILL).

It took a while for this new way of entering cataloging information into computer records to catch on, but gradually more MARC records were made and more computer programs were designed around them. Nowadays, most libraries, no matter how small, already have or are in the process of getting integrated library systems with modules for acquisitions, serials tracking, cataloging, an online catalog, and circulation—and all these modules share the same MARC records for their different functions.

Let us consider the wonder of MARC for a (not so) brief moment.

The MARC standards that were developed in the United States (first called LCMARC, then USMARC) morphed into slightly different standards when they were implemented in other countries, becoming AUSMARC, CANMARC, UKMARC, and so on. Over time, however, most of these variations were either dropped or harmonized with the original format to produce what is now called MARC 21. MARC 21 is currently maintained by the Library of Congress, the Library and Archives Canada (formerly National Library of Canada), the British Library, and committees of the library associations of the United States and Canada: MARBI and CCM, respectively.

Because we collected more than just books in our libraries, different groups of specialist catalogers developed special formats for different types of materials. For a number of years, this meant that we dealt with slightly different MARC codes for books, visual materials (e.g., videos, graphics), maps, sound recordings, music, serials, and so on. In a massive undertaking called *format integration*, which was almost as difficult as coming up with the standards in the first place, all the discrepancies between the formats for different materials were eliminated, giving us a unified set of standards for the coding of the bibliographic information for anything we need to catalog.

You can purchase the most current version of the MARC standards from LC in print form (*MARC 21 Format for Bibliographic Data*, or MARC), and you can find a concise version online (*MARC 21 Concise Format for Bibliographic Data*). OCLC offers its own online version of the standards, complete and unabridged, and with many good examples and explanations (*OCLC Bibliographic Formats and Standards*).

No sooner did we get the standards for bibliographic information nicely set up than we discovered we needed to code more than just bibliographic information for our library automation systems. As mentioned earlier, part 2 of AACR2 tells about providing access points or headings to allow patrons to search our catalogs and find descriptions of our resources. These headings must be entered consistently if we want patrons to find everything in one place. To make headings consistent, we apply something we call *authority control*. One very important aspect of authority control is supplying the cross-references that take patrons from headings we don't use (such as Dr. Seuss) to headings we do use (such as Seuss, Dr.).

> *Dr. Seuss. Author
> **SEE** <u>Seuss, Dr.</u> **Matches 66 Items**

We enter cross-references into MARC authority records, not MARC bibliographic records (see chapter 5).

We also have MARC formats for holdings information (bar code numbers and notes about specific books, videos, or other cataloged items), community information (such as the location and dates of the local chamber of commerce or Kiwanis Club meetings), and classification information (used by the publishers of the classification schemes). This introductory chapter will not go into any more detail about these other formats, but some of the readings that follow this chapter explain them further.

As you can tell by now, a lot is going on in this process we call cataloging. In the remainder of this chapter, our task is to concentrate on the part about providing bibliographic description. It sounds simple, but don't forget that bibliographic description relies on strict adherence to two complicated and ever-changing standards—AACR and MARC—as well as more detailed explanations that help catalogers apply the standards uniformly.[5]

That's enough of the history and reasons why cataloging is how it is, so let us boldly dive into the deep end. The bottom line is that AACR tells us what bibliographic information to provide, and then MARC tells us how to code it for the computer. You could, if you wished, use MARC and not follow AACR2, or follow AACR2 and not use MARC, but neither of these options would be a good idea for a small library. Leave such courage to the cutting-edge folks. If you want to copy cataloging from others or have others do your cataloging or both, your records must follow both AACR2 and MARC.

The Cataloging Process

Here's how it works: Picture me with a book or video, or some other fascinating library resource in one hand. See me start flipping through AACR2 with the other hand. I begin at part 1, chapter 1 (begin at the beginning, we always say).

Chapter 1 tells me how to describe any type of material or resource I might encounter in my library. That sounds like a pretty useful set of rules, so why look any further? It's all in the history. Chapter 1 was written way back when we only cataloged books. Videos, sound recordings, serials, and so on have special features that chapter 1 does not cover. I have to turn to chapters 2–12 for instructions that help me to describe different types of materials (e.g., chapter 2 for books, chapter

7 for videos). The first thing to remember about AACR2 is always begin with the general descriptive rules and then turn to the appropriate special rules chapter to see if there are other important details you need to know.

Whatever I am describing, chapter 1 tells me to break my description of it down into eight broad *areas of information*. Instructions for providing the information for these eight areas are given in numbered subrules in chapter 1 and in similarly numbered subrules in chapters 2–12. Now it's time to pull out the MARC manual. There I see each of the areas of information are *fields* in MARC records.

Figure 3-1 illustrates how it all fits together. Instructions for entering information for the "Title and statement of responsibility" area can be found in AACR2 rule 1.1 (for all materials), 2.1 (for books), 6.1 (for sound recordings), 7.1 (for videos), or 12.1 (for serials). Then MARC says to put the title and statement of responsibility information in a 245 field. Look closely at figure 3-1 and see where MARC says to put each of the eight areas of information.

Figure 3-1.   Relationship of AACR2 Rules and MARC 21 Fields

AACR2	ALL	Book	Sound	Video	Serial	MARC 21 Fields
	Ch 1	*Ch 2*	*Ch 6*	*Ch 7*	*Ch 12*	
General rules	1.0	2.0	6.0	7.0	12.0	
Areas of information						
Title and statement of responsibility area	1.1	2.1	6.1	7.1	12.1	245
Edition area	1.2	2.2	6.2	7.2	12.2	250
Material/Type of publication specific details area	1.3				12.3	various
Publication, distribution, etc. area	1.4	2.4	6.4	7.4	12.4	260
Physical description area	1.5	2.5	6.5	7.5	12.5	300
Series area	1.6	2.6	6.6	7.6	12.6	4XX[a]
Note area	1.7	2.7	6.7	7.7	12.7	5XX
Standard number and terms of availability area	1.8	2.8	6.8	7.8	12.8	02X

[a] 4XX means any field bearing a tag beginning with 4 (e.g., 440 or 490); 5XX means any field bearing a tag beginning with 5 (e.g., 502, 504, 505).

No doubt about it, these cataloging rules are detailed! The next thing you need to know about them is that they even tell you exactly where to look on the resource for the information that you are to use to describe the resource. If I am describing a book, for example, chapter 2 tells me where to look on the book for the information for each of the areas shown in figure 3-1. Note that you look in the specific chapters (2–12) rather than the general chapter (1) for instructions on these "sources of information." Figure 3-2 shows you some examples of these instructions.

Okay, you've got it that you have to divide the bibliographic description of a resource into areas of information, and the information for those areas must come from specific places on the resource. That's the first step. Once you have that idea, the rules take you one step deeper, because each area of information is further subdivided into *elements*. These elements become *subfields* in MARC records.

Figure 3-2.   AACR2 Prescribed Sources for Different Formats

AACR2	Book	Sound
	Ch 2	*Ch 6*
Title and statement of responsibility area	Title page	Physical carrier and labels
Edition area	Title page, other preliminaries, colophon	Physical carrier and labels, accompanying textual material, container (box)
Publication, distribution, etc. area	Title page, other preliminaries, colophon	Physical carrier and labels, accompanying textual material, container (box)
Physical description area	The whole publication	Any source
Series area	Series title page, monograph title page, cover, rest of publication	Physical carrier and labels, accompanying textual material, container (box)
Note area	Any source	Any source
Standard number and terms of availability area	Any source	Any source

Figure 3-3 illustrates how the "Title and statement of responsibility" area is divided into elements. It shows that you will find the instructions for entering the information for the "Title proper" element in rule AACR2 1.1B (for all materials), 2.1B (for books), 6.1B (for sound recordings), 7.1B (for videos), and 12.1B (for serials), and so on. Then MARC says to put that information in a subfield a in the 245 field. The figure goes on to reveal that you will find the instructions for entering the information for the *general material designation* (GMD) element in rule 1.1C (for all materials), 2.1C (for books), 6.1C (for sound recordings), 7.1C (for videos), 12.1C (for serials), and so on. Then MARC says to put that information in a subfield h in the 245 field. I could continue, but I'm sure you get the picture.

Remember I said that the rules tell you *where* to look on the resource for the descriptions to put in each area of information? Add to that: down at the element level, the rules also tell you exactly *how* to enter each piece of information. Once you go to the right place on a resource to find a particular piece of information, the rules then tell you whether to give that information

exactly as it is given on the resource (e.g., titles, parallel titles, and subtitles) in the form in which it appears (e.g., statements of responsibility);

Figure 3-3.   AACR2 Rules and MARC 21 Format Subfields

AACR2	ALL	Book	Sound	Video	Serial	MARC 21 Subfield
	Ch 1	*Ch 2*	*Ch 6*	*Ch 7*	*Ch 12*	
Title and statement of responsibility area	1.1	2.1	6.1	7.1	12.1	245
Preliminary rule	1.1A	2.1A	6.1A	7.1A	12.1A	
Title proper	1.1B	2.1B	6.1B	7.1B	12.1B	$a
General material designation	1.1C	2.1C	6.1C	7.1C	12.1C	$h
Parallel titles	1.1D	2.1D	6.1D	7.1D	12.1D	$b
Other title information	1.1E	2.1E	6.1E	7.1E	12.1E	$b
Statements of responsibility	1.1F	2.1F	6.1F	7.1F	12.1F	$c
Items without a collective title	1.G	2.G	6.G	7.G	12.G	$b or $c

as found but using abbreviations from appendix B and numerals from appendix C (edition statements and publication details); or

as free text (notes).

The makers of the rules aren't intentionally trying to drive you crazy, no matter how it seems. Keep that in mind as we go to the next level of detail, because the rules then proceed to tell us exactly what punctuation to put in front of or around each element/subfield in each area/field.

This punctuation is called *ISBD punctuation* and can be very useful for patrons, even kids. If you are looking at a record in your catalog and trying to help someone figure out the title of a resource when that title is in a language you cannot read, just look for one of the ISBD punctuation marks that signals where the title ends and some other sort of information begins. For example, suppose the catalog record says, "Rawls : een inleiding in zijn werk / Ronald Tinnevelt & Gert Verschraegen." Using the ISBD punctuation, you can break this title and statement of responsibility area/field into its elements/subfields, as follows:

"Rawls" is the main title, because it is at the beginning of the field.

"een inleiding in zijn werk" is the subtitle (preceded by space, colon, space).

"Ronald Tinnevelt & Gert Verschraegen" is the statement of responsibility (preceded by space slash space).

Granted, your smaller patrons might find them hard to remember, but you should not find it too difficult to grasp the punctuation rules.

Many patterns are found in the rules. These patterns may help you to see the big picture, but there's no escaping the need to get down to nitty-gritty details and learn the actual rules. It might be helpful to start with Michael Gorman's *Concise AACR* or *Maxwell's Handbook for AACR2* or both, and then move up to Deborah A. Fritz's *Cataloging with AACR2 and MARC21*.[6] Eventually, though, you still have to face the full versions of rules and standards. Let's see more examples of how they work together.

More about MARC

We have touched on MARC, showing how areas of information are entered into MARC fields, and elements of these areas are entered into MARC subfields. The same information we once entered on cards, we now enter in MARC records. Figure 3-4 illustrates how areas and elements from a card display become fields and subfields in a MARC display.

Figure 3-4.　Card-Style and MARC 21 Format–Style Records

Main entry.
　　Title [GMD] : subtitle / statement of responsibility ; another statement of
responsibility. -- Edition statement. -- Place : Publisher, Date.

　　Extent of item : other physical details ; dimensions + accompanying
material. -- (Series statement)

　　Notes.
　　ISBN

　　1. LC subject heading. 2. Juvenile subject heading. I. Additional author
added entry. II. Title added entry. III. Series added entry.
　　　　　　　　　　　　　　　　　　　　　　　　　　　　　　　LCCN

010		‡aLCCN
020		‡aISBN
1XX	1	‡aMain entry.
245	10	‡aTitle‡h[GMD] :‡bsubtitle /‡cstatement of responsibility.
250		‡aEdition statement.
260		‡aPlace :‡bPublisher,‡cDate.
300		‡a Extent of item :‡b other physical details ;‡ dimensions +‡eaccompanying material.
4XX	0	‡aSeries statement
5XX		‡aNotes.
6XX	0	‡aLC subject heading.
6XX	1	‡aJuvenile subject heading.
7XX	1	‡aAdditional author added entry.
8XX	1	‡aSeries added entry.

If you try to match each phrase from the card to the MARC record, you'll notice the Title Added Entry on the card seems to be missing in the MARC record. Actually, it is present in the coding. The first indicator in the 245 field (the 1 after the 245 tag) tells your OPAC software to make a Title Added Entry. I'll explain indicators, field, tags, and other MARC coding terms shortly.

Take a deep breath and grit your teeth; this may not be fun, but trust me, you need to know this stuff.

A MARC record begins with a *leader*, which tells a computer program what kind of data the record that follows contains, and a *directory*, which tells the program where to find everything in the record. The leader and directory are followed by the cataloging data, and all of this is stored as one long string of characters. If you have ever saved a record in "MARC Format" from the LC OPAC, you will have seen the leader, directory, and long string of data in its raw "communications" format. Figure 3-5 is an example of a record saved in MARC format from the LC OPAC. Fortunately, when we catalogers look at MARC, it is displayed in a more readable manner, as shown in figure 3-6.

Figure 3-5.   MARC Record from the LC OPAC Displayed
in Raw Communications Format

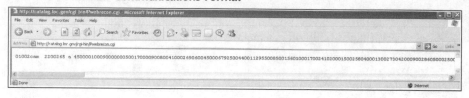

Figure 3-6.   MARC Record from the LC OPAC Displayed in MARC Format

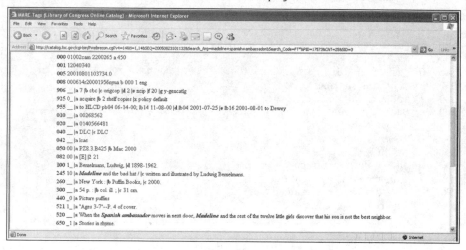

We need fields for entering the different areas of information required by the cataloging rules. In MARC, each field is labeled with a *tag*. Tags are three-digit numbers used to tell programs (and catalogers) what kind of information the field contains. For example, the 245 tag indicates the field that follows contains title and statement of responsibility information; the 260 tag indicates the field that follows contains publishing information.

These fields can be further subdivided into *subfields* for entering the specific elements of each area of information. In MARC, each subfield uses a code to tell programs (and catalogers) what kind of information the subfield contains. For example, subfield a in the 245 field contains the title, and subfield c in the 245 field contains the statement of responsibility.

Because subfield codes use letters of the alphabet (in lowercase) and the numerals 1 through 9, MARC needs a way to differentiate a subfield code from the actual data in a field. This is done using a subfield *delimiter*. The delimiter is a special code that tells the program (and the cataloger) that the character that follows is a subfield code. A delimiter can look different depending on the software: in the LC example in figures 3-4 and 3-5, it is a pipe sign "|"; in OCLC, it looks like a double dagger "‡"; in ITS, it looks like an upside-down highlighted triangle "▼"; in many other displays, it looks like a dollar sign "$." However it might look, it is the same special character in all cases (ASCII 1F in hex or ASCII 31 in decimal). Be sure to follow your software's instructions for entering this character rather than trying to enter any of the above symbols—never enter a dollar sign ($) as a subfield delimiter.

In addition to the tag and the subfield codes, each variable data field has two important codes called *indicators*. The meaning of each indicator depends on the field to which it is attached. Indicators can tell us

> whether a field should be indexed (traced);
>
> whether a field should be displayed (printed);
>
> whether any characters at the beginning of the field should be skipped in indexing (nonfiling characters);
>
> whether a special label should be displayed (printed) for the field (display constants); and
>
> other equally important things.

It is very important that indicator positions are coded correctly. If they are wrong, your kids might not be able to find books by their titles (because an indicator told the system to start indexing at an inappropriate place in the title), or they might not be able to understand why a particular record is displayed from their search (because an indicator told the software to index a field but not display it). Figure 3-7 illustrates the main sections of a variable data field (010–9XX).

Control fields (001–009) are an exception to this pattern. They do not have indicators or subfields. Control fields may contain only a single data element, such as a control number (001), a control number identifier (003), or a timestamp (005), or they may contain a series of alphanumeric codes (006, 007, and 008).

Figure 3-7.   Main Sections of a Variable Data Field (010–9XX)

Tag	1st Indicator	2nd Indicator	Subfield a	Subfield b	Subfield c
245	1	0	$a Title	$b subtitle	$c responsibility

Although difficult for beginners to remember, these coded fields are important. For example, it is a coded field that tells your software to show a little CD icon when a record is describing a sound recording. If the coded field that does this is not entered (as is so often the case), the displayed icon will be for a book (the default); or, if you are looking for all of your books in Spanish but have not coded the language code for Spanish, your software cannot identify those books.

As with AACR, there are patterns in MARC coding. For example, fields are grouped into blocks of tags, as shown in figure 3-8. Patterns also occur across groupings. For example, all personal name headings are entered in tags that end in 00; all corporate name headings are entered in tags that end in 10; and so on, as shown in figure 3-9.

Figure 3-8.   MARC Format Field Tag Groups

001–009	Control fields
01X–04X	Number and code fields
05X–08X	Classification and call number fields
1XX	Main entry fields
20X–24X	Title and title-related fields
250–270	Edition, imprint, etc. fields
3XX	Physical description, etc. fields
4XX	Series statement fields
5XX	Note fields
6XX	Subject access fields
70X–75X	Added entry fields
76X–78X	Linking entry fields
80X–83X	Series added entry fields
841–88X	Holdings, location, alternate graphs, etc. fields
9XX	Local fields

Figure 3-9.   Groupings across MARC Field Tags

X00	Personal name headings
X10	Corporate name headings
X11	Conference name headings
X30	Uniform title headings

From figures 3-7 and 3-8 we can discern the following:

A personal name heading that is a main entry is entered in a 100 field (1XX = main entry; X00 = personal name).

A corporate name heading that is a subject is entered in a 610 field (6XX = subject heading; X10=corporate name).

A conference that is an added entry is entered in a 711 field (7XX = added entry; X11 = conference name).

A uniform title that is a series added entry is entered in an 830 field (8XX = series added entry; X30 = uniform title), or a 440—but that's another story.

Patterns also occur within each grouping. For example, the second indicator of all 6XX fields tells us the source of the subject heading entered in that field (e.g., LCSH, Annotated Children's, Sears). All the fields in the 6XX also share the same subfields, as shown in figure 3-10. Any of the subject subdivision subfields can be added to any subject heading in a 6XX field.

There is a great deal more that you should learn about MARC coding. Two very good places to start would be the LC tutorial called *Understanding MARC Bibliographic* and Fritz's *MARC21 for Everyone.*

This short chapter cannot begin to teach you all you need to know to create a MARC 21 record following AACR2. To illustrate, let's walk through the steps of how a cataloger would apply AACR2 and MARC 21 to provide the title and statement of responsibility area of information for a book:

1. Turn to AACR2 to

    find out where to look on the book to find the title and statement of responsibility information (the title page—2.0B);

    check the general rules for titles (1.1B);

    check the book rules for titles (2.1B);

Figure 3-10.   Patterns within Groupings

$v	Form subdivision
$x	General subdivision
$y	Chronological subdivision
$z	Geographic subdivision

find out what to enter first (the title proper—1.1B1); and

check whether to transcribe the title exactly as given or with abbreviations, and so on (transcribe exactly—1.1B2).

2. With the title ready for entering, turn to MARC, which tells you to

enter 245 as the field tag (to tell the program you are about to provide
title information);

skip the first indicator—until you know how you are going to index the
title (as a main entry or an added entry);

look at the first word of the title and decide whether you want to begin
indexing at that word, or skip it (if the word is an initial article,
such as *The, An, A, Los, Las,* and so on, enter the number of characters the program is to skip before beginning indexing in the second
indicator; if the word is not an initial article, enter 0);

enter subfield a (because title information in this field always begins
with the title proper), not forgetting the special delimiter character
(which could display as ‡, ▼, $, etc.); and

enter the title proper, transcribed exactly as it is given on the title page,
just as AACR said to do.

3. Alternate between AACR and MARC to complete the title field:

Read on through the rules to find the next bit of information that you
might need to provide: a GMD (general material designation), what
the resource is, generally speaking—you have a book and it is not
large print, so you do not need a GMD, so skip it.

The next rule says to look for a Parallel title—your book is not bilingual
(e.g., with two titles, one in English and one in Spanish), so skip
this too.

The next rule says to look for Other title information, such as a subtitle—yes, you have one of those; you already know where to look for
the subtitle (the same place as the title, i.e., the title page, per 2.0B),
so read the general rules (1.1E), check how you are to transcribe it
(1.1E2), and check for any special book rules (2.1E); then enter it—
but where?

MARC says subtitles go in tag 245 subfield b; but what about the special
separating punctuation (the ISBD punctuation)?

Go back to AACR, which says a subtitle is preceded by a colon (1.1A1).

Enter the subtitle in a subfield b preceded by a colon, transcribing it exactly as given on the title page, just as AACR said to do.

The next AACR rule says to look for a Statement of responsibility— your book has an author and an illustrator; you already know where to look for this information (the same place as the title—the title page, 2.0B), so just check how to transcribe it (1.1F2), read the general rules (1.1F), and check for any special book rules (2.1F); then enter it—where?

MARC says statements of responsibility go in tag 245 subfield c; but what about the special separating punctuation (the ISBD punctuation)?

Go back to AACR, which says that a statement of responsibility is preceded by a forward slash, and different functions (e.g., author and illustrator) are separated by space semicolon space (1.1A1).

You have two statements of responsibility (author and illustrator), so you have to check MARC again for whether you need two subfields c—no, subfield c is not repeatable in the 245 field.

Enter the statement of responsibility in a single subfield c preceded by a slash, separating the different statements with space semicolon space, and transcribing the statements exactly as they are given on the title page, just as AACR said to do.

Finally, add the end of field punctuation: a new area of information is going to follow this field, and because AACR says all new areas are preceded by period, space, dash, space (1.0C1), this field must end with a period (the computer will provide the space dash space if it is needed).

There you have it—how to enter the title and statement of responsibility for a book into a MARC 21 bibliographic record, in a nutshell. Should you wish to know how to enter an edition statement, publication details, the physical description, series statements, notes, and standard numbers—in other words, the rest of the bibliographic description for your book—you should sign up as soon as you can for a continuing education workshop on the subject. You probably have already guessed that this isn't something you can learn by reading manuals on your own or by trial and error. There are too many layers to sort through without some sort of guidance.

Don't think that you can escape your fate by farming it out to someone else. You still have to know something about it all to maintain quality control over the records you are sent. And you do need quality control, because not even LC catalogers are perfect.

All that said, do not despair. It isn't that hard to grasp all this once someone explains it to you. Once you've grasped it, you'll be able to provide your kids with an effective catalog that will perform its function of making your library's resources accessible to those kids, their parents, and anyone else who stumbles upon it.

Notes

1. *Anglo-American Cataloguing Rules*, 2nd ed., 2002 rev. and updates (Chicago: American Library Association, 2002–).
2. Joint Steering Committee for Revision of AACR, "A Brief History of AACR," http://www .collectionscanada.ca/jsc/history.html#top.
3. International Standard Bibliographic Description (ISBD) is a program sponsored by the International Federation of Library Associations and Organizations (IFLA). ISBD regulates four things: the areas that comprise an internationally recognized standard bibliographic description; the order in which the areas appear in a catalog record; the sources from which the information for these areas should be taken; and how each area and subarea are to be identified by using special punctuation marks. Don't confuse ISBD with ISBN (International Standard Book Number), though they sound very similar. The ISBN is a unique identifier assigned by publishers to each of the books they issue. If assigned, ISBNs are included in bibliographic descriptions in part of the eighth area of description.
4. See chapters 6, 7, and 8 for explanations of Library of Congress Annotated Card program subject headings for children's materials, *Sears List of Subject Headings*, and *Dewey Decimal Classification*, respectively.
5. These include *Library of Congress Rule Interpretations* (2002 cumulation, plus updates for 2003, 2004, and 2005), available on *Cataloger's Desktop*, http://www.loc.gov/cds/desktop; the *CONSER Cataloging Manual, CONSER Editing Guide*, http://www.loc.gov/cds/ catman.html#saf; and other manuals issued by the Library of Congress.
6. Michael Gorman, *Concise AACR2* (Chicago: American Library Association, 2004); Robert L. Maxwell, *Maxwell's Handbook for AACR2* (Chicago: American Library Association, 2004); and Deborah A. Fritz, *Cataloging with AACR2 and MARC21* (Chicago: American Library Association, 2003).

Recommended Reading

Fritz, Deborah A. *MARC21 for Everyone: A Practical Guide*. Chicago: American Library Association, 2003.

MARC 21 Concise Format for Bibliographic Data. 2003 concise ed. http://www.loc.gov/marc/ bibliographic/ecbdhome.html.

MARC 21 Format for Bibliographic Data (MARC). http://www.loc.gov/marc/bibliographic/ ecbdhome/html.

OCLC Bibliographic Formats and Standards. 1993. http://www.oclc.org/bibformats/en.

Understanding MARC Bibliographic. 2000. 5th ed. http://www.loc.gov/marc/umb.

4

Copy Cataloging Correctly

Deborah A. Fritz

Background

Having read this far, you may now know just enough about AACR2, MARC 21, descriptive cataloging, authority controlled headings, subject headings, call numbers, and the special joys of cataloging nonprint material to realize you'd rather not do it yourself if you don't have to. Another way to get your cataloging done is to copy someone else's records. This is perfectly acceptable—even encouraged—behavior in the cataloging world. In fact, library administrators seem to believe the glorious day has already arrived when anyone in the library can catalog, because someone else, somewhere else, has already made a record for every resource in the world. All a cataloger has to do these days is find and copy those records. Would that it were so simple!

Let's go back to the beginning (again) to set the stage for how copy cataloging fits into the whole cataloging picture. You have a stack of new items: books, videos, DVDs, and so on. You need to get those resources out on the shelves. But before you can put them on the shelves, they need to be cataloged. This means you must

> describe each item (bibliographic description, e.g., title, edition, publisher, etc.);
>
> provide terms by which someone might search for the item (access points, e.g., names, titles, subjects, etc.);

This chapter is based on material presented at the author's workshop "Just for Copy Cats" and is provided here by permission of the author.

provide a call number (classification) so that each item can be shelved with other materials on similar subjects (e.g., ships), or with other materials of the same physical medium (e.g., large print); and

link the bar code number on the item to the catalog record (holdings information).

This detailed information has to be entered into MARC records so your OPAC can show it to your kids, your circulation system can track loans accurately, and you can share your records and resources with other libraries.

How can it be done? Original cataloging is time consuming and demands a high level of training. Copy cataloging is cost-effective and does not require quite as much training. However, to do a proper job of copy cataloging, at the very least you have to know the following:

- where to find records to copy
- how to search for records to copy
- how to match records with your resources
- how to edit records
- how to add holdings information, such as bar code numbers, locations, and call numbers, to the records
- how to download records from the source computer
- how to import records to your library automation system

I can't tell you about the last three steps. How you download from your source of MARC records depends on what the source is. How you import records to your library automation system is up to that automation system. How you add holdings information is also up to your library automation system. I can and will, however, tell you something about the first four steps.

Sources of MARC Records

There are many records out there that you can copy instead of having to create your own—you just have to find them. Here's a list of some sources of MARC records:

Shared systems. If you share a database with other libraries, and another library has already added to the database a MARC record that matches your resource, you simply have to attach your holdings information (bar code, call number, item cost, etc.) to that record; this may be called *add item* or *linking*, but it is still copy cataloging.

Library of Congress. The online public access catalog (OPAC) of the Library of Congress, http://catalog.loc.gov. You can copy records from LC's OPAC and import them into your own library automation system.

Bibliographic utilities. Bibliographic utilities, such as OCLC (http://www.oclc .org) or RLIN (the Research Libraries Information Network, http://www.rlg.org). If you are a member of such a utility, you can copy records made by other members (including LC).

MARC record vendors. MARC record vendors offer access to copies of the LC database via CD-ROMs or the Internet or both; MARC records collected from other sources may also be included.

Z39.50 software. If the cataloging module of your automation system offers Z39.50 capability, you can use it to search the databases of hundreds of library systems via the Internet and download MARC records from those databases; if the cataloging module in your library system does not offer Z39.50, you can buy stand-alone software to obtain the same capability.

Outsourcing. Many libraries contract with book jobbers and publishers to receive a MARC record for every resource that they purchase.

Notice that I include outsourcing in my list of options for copy cataloging. Outsourcing is described in more detail in chapter 13, but be aware it is a type of copy cataloging, and you will have to check the records you receive just as though you were pulling them in from any other source. Outsourcing saves the step of finding the records. Please don't think that once you get your outsourced records all you have to do is load them. You might have to do this and hope for the best if you are doing a retrospective conversion (i.e., converting a card catalog to MARC records) or if you are getting fifty thousand records all at once for an opening day collection. But, if you are receiving small numbers of vendor records on an ongoing basis for the new materials you order, you need to check them to be sure that they truly match your resources, and to see if they need editing.

I'll get to matching and editing shortly, but first let's consider some secrets of searching.

Searching for MARC Records

I listed a number of options for sources of MARC records earlier. Unfortunately, each of these sources has its own quirks when it comes to searching. You'll have to read the instructions for each source of records to learn the quirks. Don't be like the cataloger who came to one of my workshops and revealed that for five years she hadn't been able to find any records for ISBNs that ended with an X. The instruction manual for her software had the answer (enter 7 instead of X), but she hadn't read it!

You have to find out what your cataloging interface requires when it comes to searching. Here are a few suggestions for what you might want to research:

Do you search as you see (e.g., just enter a title as it is on the book), or do you use search keys such as OCLC's 3,2,2,1 for a *derived key* title search?

Do you include hyphens when searching via an LCCN or ISBN?

Are there *stopwords* that you should not include in your search?

Do you enter or omit punctuation such as apostrophes, commas, and so on?

Read your software manuals for the answers to these and similar questions.

Once you know how your search software works, you need to learn the best search terms to use for finding matching MARC records, no matter what your source. Some search terms are great for finding any type of record (for example, ISBNs are good for finding records for books, videos, sound, etc.). Some are extremely useful for certain types of material but not for others (LCCNs are good for books and print serials, but unavailable for videos and sound; on the other hand, publisher's numbers are great for videos and sound, but not helpful for books or serials). Still others can be used for any type of material, but only if other search terms fail (such as series titles).

To keep things simple and brief, this chapter covers only search terms for finding book records. For more details on search terms for electronic resources, sound, videos, and serials, see the Search Tables in Deborah A. Fritz's *Cataloging with AACR2 and MARC21*.[1]

Searching LCCNs

An LCCN is usually found on a title page verso (if it is present on a book at all) and will appear in one of two formats, depending on when the number was assigned:

> *Old format (pre-2001):* for example, 96-16774
>
> *New format (post-2001):* for example, 2001-456 (all four digits representing the year, not just the final two digits, are used for the first part of the number)

An LCCN is a very good choice for searching. If you search the LC database by an LCCN, you should bring up only one record. Usually, this record will match your resource. However, be warned that an LCCN search in any database other than LC's can sometimes bring up more than one record. When an LCCN retrieves multiple records, or retrieves a record that does not match your resource, you must flag that LCCN for possible editing later.

Searching ISBNs

An ISBN is usually found on a title page verso or the back cover of a book or both, and may take one of two forms, depending on when it was assigned:

Old format (pre-2004): ten digits (the last digit can be X, but no other alphabetic characters are valid)

New format (post-2004): ten or thirteen digits (the last digit can be X, but no other alphabetic characters are valid)

An ISBN is very important for searching. If you search by an ISBN, most of the time you will bring up just one record that matches your book. That record may not always match your resource, however, or it might retrieve multiple records; in either of those cases you must flag that ISBN for possible editing later.

Searching Names

Names can be searched, but only if other terms do not work, because they are less efficient as search terms. The name you search does not have to be an author. It could be the name of an illustrator, an editor, a translator, and so on. Be careful how you search for compound surnames, because they can be tricky. For example, how would you search for Lynn Reid Banks—as "Banks, Lynn Reid" or as "Reid Banks, Lynn"? Also, watch for authors who have changed their names or have used more than one name (several pseudonyms or a pseudonym and a real name).

Searching Titles

If a title is unique, it can be an effective search term, especially when numbers, such as LCCNs or ISBNs, are unavailable. Titles can sometimes be much simpler to search than names. However, different authors have been known to use the same title for very different books, so never assume a record found by a title search is sure to match your book.

Searching Combined Names/Titles

Combining names and titles (if your search menu will let you do so) can be much more effective than searching either by names or titles alone. You do not have to use the name of an author for this type of search; you can also use the name of an editor, illustrator, or the like.

Searching Series Titles

Sometimes nothing seems to work, but you know there must be a record somewhere for your resource. If there is a series title on the resource, try searching it. You may get a long list of works in the series, but it still might be better than trying to search by a common name, such as "Smith, John" or "Shakespeare, William," or a common title, such as *The Civil War* (which retrieves 3,300 different records when searched in LC's OPAC).

Search Qualifiers

Dates

If you have a date on your resource, you can narrow your search by adding the date, if your software will allow you to do so. You may have to go to a more advanced level of searching to do this.

Physical Format

There is little point in qualifying by "type of material = book" because most records in library catalogs are still for books. However, if you are looking for the sound recording of *Hamlet* rather than the book, qualifying by the type of material could narrow your results very nicely.

Matching MARC Records against Resources

Once you have found a record, you cannot simply say, "That looks close enough" and use it, or change a few things to make it match better and then use it. You need to review a list of *match criteria* to be sure that the record you have found truly matches the resource in your hand.

Until the end of 2004, the only official match criteria documentation available was provided by OCLC in its online manual.[2] The guidelines in this rather long chapter are paraphrased in a series of shorter tables in Fritz's *Cataloging with AACR2 and MARC21*. In late 2004, the Task Force on an Appendix of Major and Minor Changes (part of the Committee on Cataloging: Description and Access of the Cataloging and Classification Section of the Association for Library Collections and Technical Services) produced its own set of guidelines in a document called *Differences Between, Changes Within*.[3]

The guidelines in the three documents just listed are basically the same, just given in different forms. It doesn't really matter which set of guidelines you use, but you need to follow one of them consistently to be sure that you only copy records that really match your resources.

Why? Let's say you understand the general principles of matching records to resources, and instead of following any of the guidelines, you just do what seems good sense at the moment. One day you find a record that has the same title as your book, and the same author. The publisher is almost the same but has a slightly different name (because it was recently bought by another publisher and their names are now combined). The pagination is also slightly different, off by six pages. Because the date of publication is the same, however, you decide this record is close enough to be called a match for your resource. Meanwhile, the three sets of guidelines listed earlier all agree in saying that this record is not a match and that you need to make a new record because the name of the publisher has changed, the pagination does not match, and, if you look more closely, your book does not have the introduction mentioned in the record. Not knowing about this level of detail in matching, you take the record, change the publisher to the name on your book, and change the pagination to match yours. You may or may not remember to get rid of the wording about the introduction.

Now the record works fine in your own catalog. But are you a part of any sort of resource sharing arrangement, whether it is a union catalog, such as OCLC, RLIN, or SUNLINK, or a virtual catalog? If you are, or think you might be someday, then picture what happens when your record joins other records in the union catalog. Because your record has the same LCCN/ISBN as the record you copied and changed, your record will be linked to that original record. One day a student, John, searches and finds the record to which you are linked, and requests it from your library to write a paper. John gets your version of the work, finds it lacks the introduction (which is really what he was looking for), and is now up the creek— with no time to go back to the library to get the version he really needs. He loses all faith in the ILL process, decides to purchase the item, and never darkens the door of a library again, all because you did not follow the guidelines for matching records.

Wouldn't it be better to follow the match criteria guidelines than to lose this patron forever?

When matching records, always be sure to look at the MARC record view. Don't try to get by with a labeled view, and never rely on a brief view, such as the one shown in figure 4-1, taken from LC's OPAC. It may look like the brief view shows plenty of information, but a number of the fields that you are supposed to check when matching are not displayed. Even the full view of an OPAC lacks some data you need for matching. Figure 4-2 shows a full record display from the LC OPAC. It appears to be comprehensive, but it hides some important coded information needed for matching. No matter what source you copy from, use the MARC view, shown in figure 4-3, to match records to resources. The fields in bold print are used for matching.

Figure 4-1. A Brief Record from the LC OPAC

Brief Record	Subjects/Content	Full Record	MARC Tags

Henry the fourth / by Stuart J. Murphy ; illustrated by Scott Nash.

LC Control Number: 98004960

Type of Material: Text (Book, Microform, Electronic, etc.)

Brief Description: Murphy, Stuart J., 1942-
Henry the fourth / by Stuart J. Murphy ; illustrated by Scott Nash.
1st ed.
New York : HarperCollins Publishers, c1999.
33 p. : col. ill. ; 21 x 26 cm.

Links: Publisher description

CALL NUMBER: QA141.3 .M87 1999

Figure 4-2. A Full Record from the LC OPAC

Brief Record	Subjects/Content	Full Record	MARC Tags

Henry the fourth / by Stuart J. Murphy ; illustrated by Scott Nash.

LC Control Number: 98004960

Type of Material: Text (Book, Microform, Electronic, etc.)

Personal Name: Murphy, Stuart J., 1942-

Main Title: Henry the fourth / by Stuart J. Murphy ; illustrated by Scott Nash.

Edition Information: 1st ed.

Published/Created: New York : HarperCollins Publishers, c1999.

Related Names: Nash, Scott, 1959- ill.

Description: 33 p. : col. ill. ; 21 x 26 cm.

ISBN: 006027610X
0064467198 (pbk.)
0060276118 (lib. bdg.)

Summary: A simple story about four dogs at a dog show.introduces the ordinal numbers: first, second, third, and fourth.

Target audience: "Level 1, ages 3 up"--P. [4] of cover.

Subjects: Numbers, Ordinal--Juvenile literature.
Numbers, Ordinal.

Series: MathStart

LC Classification: QA141.3 .M87 1999

Dewey Class No.: 513 21

Figure 4-3. MARC Record Highlighting Fields Used for Matching

000 01185cam 2200361 a 4500

001   98004960

003 DLC

008 980109s1999   nyua j   000 0 eng

Entrd: 980109   DtSt: s Dates: 1999,   Ctry: nyu Ills: a

Audn: j   **Form:**   Cont: GPub: Conf: 0   Fest: 0

Indx: 0   M/E: LitF: 0 Biog: Lang: eng MRec: Srce:

010   ±a 98004960

020   ±a006027610X

020   ±a0064467198 (pbk.)

020   ±a0060276118 (lib. bdg.)

040   ±aDLC±cDLC±dDLC

050 00   ±aQA141.3±b.M87 1999

082 00   ±a513±221

100 1   ±aMurphy, Stuart J.,±d1942-

245 10   **±aHenry the fourth /±cby Stuart J. Murphy ; illustrated by Scott Nash.**

246 3   ±aHenry the 4th

250   **±a1st ed.**

260   **±aNew York :±bHarperCollins Publishers,±cc1999.**

300   **±a33 p. :±bcol. ill. ;±c21 x 26 cm.**

440 0   **±aMathStart**

521 1   ±a"Level 1, ages 3 up"--P. [4] of cover.

520   ±aA simple story about four dogs at a dog show introduces the ordinal
numbers: first, second, third, and fourth.

650 0   ±aNumbers, Ordinal±vJuvenile literature.

650 1   ±aNumbers, Ordinal.

700 1   ±aNash, Scott,±d1959-±eill.

856 42   ±3Publisher description±u http://www.loc.gov/catdir/description/
hc041/98004960.html

Figure 4-4 gives a brief list of the most important fields that you must check when you are matching a book against a record. Note that, contrary to the expectations of many, neither the LCCN nor the ISBN is listed in figure 4-4 as fields that are to be used for matching. They are great for searching, but do not matter for matching.

The purpose of this chapter isn't to teach all the details of how to match records. To learn more than is given here, turn to one of the previously mentioned guidelines, attend a continuing education workshop, or both. There is, however, one important code to watch for: the record's Encoding Level (the degree of completeness of the MARC record), which is position 17 in the leader. First, remember that the leader is the first tag in a record, usually represented as tag 000. Next, when you are looking for positions in a leader string, count like a computer and start at zero (0). In the leader of the record shown in figure 4-3, position 17 is blank. This means that the record is Full Level according to LC's standards: "The most complete MARC level created from information derived from an inspection of the physical item."[4]

Figure 4-4.   Fields to Check When Matching Books

Field	Description
000/17	Encoding Level
008 Form	Form of item code
245 $anp	Title
245 $h	GMD
245 $b	Subtitle / Parallel title / Subsequent title
245 $c	Responsibility
1XX/7XX	Main entry / Added entries
250 $a	Edition
260 $b	Publisher
260 $a	Place
260 $c	Date
300 $a	Extent
300 $b	Illustrations
300 $c	Size
4XX	Series
546/500	Language note
500	Edition note
500	Physical description note
505	Contents note
533	Reproduction note

If, on the other hand, position 17 had contained an 8, it would mean that the record was *CIP*, which means Cataloging in Publication. CIP records are created when a publisher either sends LC a draft of a book that hasn't been published yet or fills out a form with information about the book. LC makes a cataloging record from that draft or form and sends it to the publisher, which prints a copy of the LC record in the book when it is published. Unfortunately, CIP records are created without the finished book in hand. Anything can change—and often does—between the time the publisher sends the draft or form to LC and the time when the book is actually published. This means you should be more lenient about the match criteria for such a record. If a record is CIP, you can accept it as a match *as long as the LCCN matches* and the rest of the record looks at all like it could be for your book.

Other signs that a record is a CIP record are

> the presence of a 263 field (projected date of publication) and

> the presence of "p. cm." as the only information in the 300 field (the book hasn't been completed; therefore, the number of pages and height of the spine can't be determined and are left blank).

If none of these CIP "signs" is present, you must follow your selected set of the match criteria guidelines carefully, to determine whether the record really matches your book.

To sum up, it is *very* important that matching is done properly. Obtain a copy of the match criteria from one of the sources listed earlier. Look carefully at your resource and at any record(s) you find that might match it. Decide whether each field/subfield listed in the match criteria is okay or not okay. If a field/subfield is okay, move on to the next field/subfield. Continue in this way until you reach the end of the list. If all fields are okay, then you have a match. If any are not okay, it is not a match, and you need to find another record (or possibly even enter a new record).

Editing MARC Records

Many bosses don't want us to edit records we copy. "Don't be so picky," they say. "If it's an LC record, it must be okay," they bleat. "You don't have the time to check records," they intone, "so don't let me catch you doing it." Our advice: don't let them catch you doing it, but do it, just the same.

Here's another tragic scenario: You work your way quickly and efficiently through an entire book cart in one day, and repeat this day after day after day. Everyone is thrilled, especially your boss, who promotes you to head of cataloging. Then, the complaints start flooding in:

Why can't I find that new best seller by its title? It turns up if I search by author, but half our patrons can't spell that surname. Did you forget to check for incorrect indexing or filing indicators in the title field of the record you copied?

Where have all the Spanish books gone? I know we ordered a bunch of bilingual kids books, but I qualified a search by "language = Spanish," and I can't find the book I distinctly remember seeing on the cart last week. Did you forget to check the Language code in the 008 of the record you copied?

A patron checked out and returned a book last month, and now needs to look at it again, but I can't find it anywhere in the catalog no matter what I search. Oh dear, you must have loaded another record with the same LCCN or ISBN and overlaid that record; you really should have checked that file of outsourced records after you loaded it to be sure that none of the records matched and overlaid incorrectly!

A patron received an overdue notice for a book she would never dream of borrowing. Again, another unchecked record was loaded that caused two different records to match and the bar code for one to be added to the record for the other.

Are you getting the picture that errors in MARC records can have a negative impact on customer satisfaction? In the late 1980s, Arlene Taylor studied accuracy in CIP records and found that "46.2 percent of the sample LC records had at least one error or discrepancy from current practice somewhere in the MARC record. . . . [S]ignificant errors, defined as errors that would affect any kind of access points, were found in 19.6 percent of the records. The difficulty was that there was no way to predict which records would fall into this group without examining every record."[5] It would be nice to think things have gotten better since then, but most catalogers will assure you that does not appear to be the case. So, check the records you copy (or purchase from a vendor) and edit them as needed.

Remember, whatever the source from which you copy records, you must go to a MARC view to do your editing. Figure 4-5 shows the fields in bold print that you need to check when editing. Notice that nearly every field in the record is bolded. That's because you need to check every one of them!

Here are examples of the most important things to look out for when editing a matching record, but don't think they are a complete list. Such a list doesn't exist, but you can find more detailed instructions on editing in the editing/cloning/creating records cheat sheets in Fritz's *Cataloging with AACR2 and MARC21*.

Figure 4-5. MARC View Highlighting Fields to Be Checked for Editing

```
000 01185cam  2200361 a 4500

001        98004960

003 DLC

008 980109s1999   nyua  j    000 0 eng

Entrd:     980109    DtSt: s  Dates: 1999,      Ctry: nyu  Ills: a

Audn:  j   Form:  Cont:   GPub:   Conf: 0  Fest: 0

Indx:   0   M/E:   LitF: 0  Biog:   Lang: eng  MRec:   Srce:

010        ±a  98004960

020        ±a006027610X

020        ±a0064467198 (pbk.)

020        ±a0060276118 (lib. bdg.)

040        ±aDLC±cDLC±dDLC

042        ±alcac

050 00     ±aQA141.3±b.M87 1999

082 00     ±a513±221

100 1      ±aMurphy, Stuart J.,±d1942-

245 10     ±aHenry the fourth /±cby Stuart J. Murphy ; illustrated by Scott Nash.

246 3      ±aHenry the 4th

250        ±a1st ed.

260        ±aNew York :±bHarperCollins Publishers,±cc1999.

300        ±a33 p. :±bcol. ill. ;±c21 x 26 cm.

440  0     ±aMathStart

521 1      ±a"Level 1, ages 3 up"--P. [4] of cover.

520        ±aA simple story about four dogs at a dog show introduces the ordinal
numbers: first, second, third, and fourth.

650  0     ±aNumbers, Ordinal±vJuvenile literature.

650  1     ±aNumbers, Ordinal.

700 1      ±aNash, Scott,±d1959-±eill.

856 42     ±3Publisher description±u http://www.loc.gov/catdir/description/hc041/
98004960.html
```

Type of record (000/06). The code in this leader position must match the physical description of the item that the patron sees in the 300 field. If a record you are copying has a Type of Record code and a 300$a that do not match, the record will have to be edited so they match. You'll need to find a MARC manual to find out what codes go in the Type of Record position.

Encoding level (000/17). If the code in this leader position is an 8, the record is CIP and will need to be examined and updated from top to bottom (see the preceding explanation).

Date (008). The first date in the 008 is the one your system uses for qualifying an OPAC search by Date of publication. This date *must* match the first date in the 260$c (except for a few rare situations, such as some serials). If, in a matching record you are copying, the first 008 Date does not match the first date in the 260$c, one or the other of those dates may need to be edited (based on the date on the book, video, etc.).

Country code (008). The Country code in the 008 is what your system uses for qualifying an OPAC search by Place of publication. This Ctry code must match the place of publication that displays to patrons in the 260$a. If, in a matching record you are copying, the Ctry code does not match the place in the 260$a, then the code must be edited. The complete list of country codes can be found at http://www .loc.gov/marc/countries/cntrhome.html. The three-letter code for any state in the United States is easy to formulate: take the postal code (in lowercase) for the state and add the letter *u* (for United States) to it. For example, the code nyu is for New York State (ny) in the United States (u).

Language code (008). The Language code in the 008 is what your system uses for qualifying an OPAC search by language. This Lang code must match the language of the resource. Catalogers do not determine the Lang code by looking at the language of the title of the work, but by the language of the work itself. If, in a matching record you are copying, the Lang code does not match the language of the resource you have, then the code must be edited. The complete list of language codes can be found at http://www.loc.gov/marc/languages/langhome.html. The language codes for the most common languages are mnemonic: English = eng; Spanish = spa; French = fre; German = ger.

245 indicators. The first indicator of the 245 is *very* important. It tells the system whether to index the title. If there is no 1XX in a record, the title is the main entry. When a title is a main entry, it is automatically indexed, so you do not need a title added entry. Setting the first indicator of the 245 to 0 (245 I1 = 0) tells the system *not* to make a title added entry, because the title in the record is already indexed. If, in a matching record you are copying, no 1XX is present, but the first indicator of the 245 is 1, this indicator must be edited (changed to 0), or the title may be indexed twice in your OPAC.

If, on the other hand, there is a 1XX in a record, then the title is not the main entry. In this instance, if you want the title to be indexed, you need a "title *added entry.*" Setting the first indicator of the 245 to 1 (245 I1= 1) tells the system to make a title added entry. If, in a matching record you are copying, a 1XX is present, but the first indicator of the 245 is 0, this indicator must be edited (changed to 1) if you want an added entry for the title.

The second indicator of the 245 is also *very* important; it tells the system where to begin indexing the title. If a title begins with an article (known as an *initial article*—in English, *A, An,* or *The*) and you don't want the title indexed under that word, you have to tell the system how many characters to skip before beginning indexing.[6]

We skip initial articles in all languages, but there are some exceptions. For example, we don't skip initial articles that begin proper names such as Los Alamos, Las Animas County, and El Cid. Watch out for words that sometimes function as initial articles and other times have different roles; for example, "Die" is an initial article in German, but not in English. A list of initial articles is online at http://lcweb.loc.gov/marc/bibliographic/bdapp-e.html.

Subject heading fields (6XX). The second indicator of all subject heading fields (6XX) represents the source of the subject heading (e.g., 0 = LCSH; 1 = Annotated Children's headings; 4 = Local subject headings). Your system looks at this second indicator to determine whether to index the subject heading. For example, your system might be programmed to index Library of Congress subject headings (6XX I2 = 0), but not LC Children's headings (6XX I2 = 1). You must train yourself to check the value of this second indicator in each 6XX of a record to make sure the record has subject headings that will be indexed in your system. If, in any matching record you are copying, none of the subject headings is indexed by your system, you need to add subject headings that will be indexed. Do this by consulting your subject heading authority and adding the headings in new 6XX fields, with the appropriate indicators. (And no, you cannot just change the indicator!)

These examples provide a taste of what you need to know and illustrate why you really do have to edit records, but they are only a taste. Much more could be covered. The indicators for the 246 are equally important (and as problematic in their own way) as the indicators for the 245. You should also watch for notes and add them if they are missing, especially those that really help kids, such as 505 Contents notes, 520 Summary notes, 521 Intended Audience notes, and 526 Study Program Information notes. This last field, 526, was added to the MARC format to make it possible to identify the curriculum with which a resource is to be used. Teachers will find it helpful, but so will kids and parents trying to find resources related to classroom subjects.

Be careful with your editing. If the only record you can find does not completely match the resource that you have, editing it to match is not the only proper option. You may need to clone a "different edition" record. This seems like editing, but it isn't, because it creates a completely new record. Because you are, in effect, creating a new record, you are no longer doing copy cataloging, which is quite a different story.

Back to the Beginning

The bottom line for copy cataloging is that you need to know the principles of cataloging to do a decent job of it. If this differs from what you've been told, then what you've been told is wrong. Familiarize yourself with the cataloging rules, the MARC standards, and the other cataloging resources described elsewhere in this book. Attend some continuing education workshops that teach the practical application of all of them. Join the AUTOCAT discussion list and ask questions, no matter how simple and rudimentary they might seem. (AUTOCAT subscribers *love* answering all questions posted on the list.) Find out if you have a local or regional cataloging special interest group (CatSIG) in your area, and, if so, join it and attend its meetings.

Whatever you do, don't make the mistake of thinking that copy cataloging is something a volunteer, a student assistant, or a typist can do without solid training—no matter how smart or educated the person might be. Outsourcing your copy cataloging helps, but you still must check the records your vendor supplies and make the vendor accountable for the quality of the records (even if you have to pay a little more for it).

Stand up for standards! Defend your database against those who say there's no need to spend time on it because everything is automated now. Proper cataloging still isn't easy, but you can do it—you just have to learn how.

Notes

1. Deborah A. Fritz, *Cataloging with AACR2 and MARC21* (Chicago: American Library Association, 2004).
2. "When to Make a New Record," Bibliographic Formats and Standards, http://www.oclc.org/bibformats/pdf/inputnewrecord.pdf.
3. *Differences Between, Changes Within* (Chicago: Association for Library Collections and Technical Services, 2004).
4. *MARC 21 Format for Bibliographic Data*, http://www.loc.gov/marc/bibliographic/ecbdldrd.html.
5. Arlene G. Taylor, *Cataloging with Copy*, 2nd ed. (Englewood, CO: Libraries Unlimited, 1988), 21.
6. To determine the number of characters to ignore in filing, count the number of letters in the word and add one character for the space that follows it. If the initial article is *The,* four characters (3 + 1) should be ignored; if it is *A,* two characters (1 + 1) should be ignored; if it is the Spanish *La,* three characters (2 + 1) should be ignored.

5

Authority Control

Kay E. Lowell

What Is Authority Control?

Authority control often is a difficult term for people to grasp. In this age of the Internet, it may be easier to understand authority control by looking at most people's experience of what it *isn't*. Do a search—any search—on the World Wide Web and you will retrieve hundreds, even thousands of hits. Many of these will leave you scratching your head, because although the term you typed may be in the page somewhere, it often has no relation to what you had in mind. The Internet has no authority control—that is, no method for assigning terms in a standardized manner.

Doris Clack, in her classic work on authority control, defines it as "the process of ensuring that every entry—name, uniform title, series, or subject—that is selected as an access point for the public catalog is unique and does not conflict, by being identical, with any other entry that is already in the catalog or that may be included at a later date."[1] Robert Maxwell describes it thus: "Authority work is so called because it deals with the formulation and recording of *authorized* heading forms in catalog records . . . to ensure consistency in the catalog so that the catalog user has to search under one and only one heading to find records associated with names, subjects, and other access points."[2]

Authority control brings together all the works by and about people who have been known by varying forms of their names or by pseudonyms or stage names. It assigns *uniform titles* to works that exist in hundreds of different versions, such as Shakespeare's works, or that are so common finding the specific one you want could be nearly impossible, such as "symphony."

Authority control directs catalogers to choose a term and define its meaning and scope, and apply it consistently whenever they catalog a work. Authority control also provides references for the users of the catalog so that if, for example, they want a book on pigs and enter that search term into a catalog using Library of Congress subject headings, the catalog will steer them gently to the word *swine*. The subject authority record often includes references to broader, narrower, and related headings, which can be invaluable to a person just beginning research in a new area of interest.

Catalogers need to understand that "we are dealing here with *access points,* not description."[3] In other words, the form of a name appearing on the title page— which is transcribed into the body of the record—may not be the authorized form of the name that appears in the main or added entries. The rules for constructing name and uniform title access points are in chapters 22 through 25 of AACR2. Guidelines for providing cross-references from one form of a name or title to another are found in chapter 26. Rules governing subject authority work are specific to the thesaurus or subject heading list being used.

Why Is Authority Control Important?

Consider this: In a card-based catalog, it is easy for the human brain to adjust for the occasional slight difference in the form of a heading. If two letters are transposed, the filer can mentally correct that error and file the card in its correct sequence. Not so with a computer, which is extremely literal. If there is a misspelling in a heading in an online catalog, the item will not be located with the rest of the works that use that access point. The item may as well not be in the collection. Likewise, if a name is entered in several different ways in an online catalog, the searcher will have to do separate searches or look in separate groups of hits to see everything the library has by or about that person—and that assumes the searcher recognizes different entries as referring to the same individual.

At a time when many libraries contribute their records to shared catalogs, and when most catalogs can be accessed remotely by anyone with a computer, authority control is even more important. Why should this be true if, as is often argued, keyword searching can meet all demands? Because, in one's home library, if a person doing a search comes across an incorrectly indexed entry or retrieves a record for no obvious reason, he or she can ask a librarian for assistance in interpreting the results. For catalog users outside the library, however, the only assistance available is provided by the cataloger who has done authority control work, adding records with explanatory notes and cross-references. Authority control, therefore, is a vital public service.

Authority Control and Children's Cataloging

For the children's catalog, the primary issue to consider is children's ability to use language. A growing body of literature reports studies of children's information-seeking behavior and their applicability to library catalogs. Paul Solomon, for example, investigated why so many of children's catalog searches fail. He found that children generally do not have the depth of knowledge needed to navigate subject headings properly, nor to make effective responses to failed searches.[4] Frances Jacobson pointed out that because the structures of bibliographic records and controlled vocabularies are highly different from and of a much higher reading level than the natural language of catalog users, children require an interpreter, guide, or mental model in order to use them.[5]

Pam Sandlian reported the results of research that prompted the creation of the CARL Corporation's Kid's Catalog product, one of the more successful graphical interfaces for children. Seventy-seven percent of children's searches on standard online catalogs failed, primarily because "children often found the language in both bibliographic records and help screens incomprehensible."[6] The Kid's Catalog, and similar products from other companies, works on the premise that a visual interface to the catalog helps children succeed where a textual interface does not. However, these products have seen only limited success, in part because the search categories represented by the icons are created by adults using adult language.

Some promising developments in the creation of a truly usable interface for children involve add-on software that uses a child's own search terms to create new interconnections between bibliographic records—a kind of custom-built authority control (see, for example, Shuyuan Zhao's dissertation of 2000).[7] However, such software is not yet widely available. For the library without access to the latest technology or programmers to implement it, one of the best tools for assisting children to use library catalogs is good, careful authority control that provides excellent cross-referencing. In fact, Solomon recommends that catalogs use local authority records or a similar input structure to build a flexible system of references based on children's language or a school's focus.

Decisions in Authority Control

As with all other areas of cataloging, decisions must be made. How will you create your authority file? Will you do your authority work in-house or purchase records from a vendor? Which subject thesaurus will you adopt? What records will you keep in your system and display to the public? How will you keep up with changes in the form of headings?

For many, if not most, libraries, budgetary constraints dictate the answers to their authority control questions. Most libraries do very little of their cataloging from scratch; rather, they purchase preexisting cataloging records through bibliographic utilities or other sources and spend their cataloging dollars on local adjustments to the records. The same can be said for authority control. Clack describes in detail the processes required to create authority records and cross-references from scratch; however, for all but the largest libraries such work is cost prohibitive. In a school library or other small library, available staff are often hard-pressed just to keep up with public services demands.

Creating the Authority File

Fortunately, there is no reason to reinvent the wheel. Thousands of large library catalogs with authority control are available for searching via the Internet. Finding the current correct form of a heading to apply to a bibliographic record is very easy. Even better, the Library of Congress's own authority files—for both adult and Annotated Card juvenile headings—are available, free of charge, at http://authorities.loc.gov. These authority records can be saved in MARC format and loaded into a local system.

A good choice for creating a library's initial authority file is to find a commercial authority control vendor and pay the vendor to do the work. Vendors can automatically replace incorrect headings with correct ones and supply matching authority records. According to the options the purchaser selects, the vendor also can apply a number of automated corrections that reflect changes in cataloging rules, bringing the bibliographic file up to current standards. This is a very worthwhile enterprise if many years have passed since the file was originally created, or if the library's collection is quite old.

An important consideration in choosing an authority vendor is whether it can supply records for the type of subject headings you use. Most vendors work with some subset of the Library of Congress headings files, supplemented with headings created by libraries or by the vendors themselves. Many also handle LC's Annotated Card headings. Fewer vendors can provide authority control for Sears subject headings, although the number is increasing. Because Sears uses a vocabulary specifically designed for very small collections and is more accessible to children than some alternatives, this increased availability is welcome.

Another thing to consider in planning authority control projects is whether your library uses more than one thesaurus, for example, regular LC subject headings for the main collection and Annotated Card headings for children's materials. If so, the local system will have to support two separate authority indexes. Because many of the headings in the Sears or Annotated Card lists are redundant, loading both types of headings into the same index will create *circular references*: instances in which one heading points to another, which points back to the original heading. This is a major disservice to your patrons. If you have no choice but to load all subject headings into one index, be prepared to do a large amount of manual cleanup to remove the circular references.

Finally, you must decide which authority records to keep in your system. Loading the entire Library of Congress subject headings file, for example, requires a system able to handle a huge file. For most libraries, a subset of headings will do. Many libraries load only those authority records that include cross-references or scope notes or both that will display and that patrons can use directly.

Do not expect perfection from an authority vendor. No matter how sophisticated the matching algorithms are, there are always names for which no authority record has ever been created, or subject headings that have changed so many times since an item was originally cataloged that no computer in the world can match it to its current authorized form. Your vendor will supply you with lists of *no-match* headings that need to be manually checked and corrected.

Maintaining the Authority File and Bibliographic Records

Work does not stop once the initial authority control project is done. Every new cataloging record needs each name, series title, uniform title, and subject heading checked against the catalog and the authority file to provide consistency and accuracy. This process can be handled in the library itself, or batches of records can be sent periodically to the authority control vendor for processing.

If your library uses a card catalog, you need to verify the accuracy of each heading as each item is cataloged. Otherwise, you will be pulling and correcting cards as headings are found to conflict with others already in the catalog. In an online catalog, there are several methods of doing ongoing authority work in-house. Records can be checked during the cataloging process, as is done with a card catalog. Many integrated library systems can provide lists of headings newly added to the catalog, which can then be checked for accuracy on a daily, weekly, or even monthly basis depending upon the volume of cataloging being done.

Some systems, because of the way they store bibliographic and authority records, are able to automatically correct headings that exactly match a *see* reference (an unused form of the heading) in an authority record as the records are loaded into the catalog. Many systems, however, have no direct linkage between a bibliographic record and its related authority records. Bibliographic records containing incorrect headings must be manually corrected, either one by one or, in some cases, via a *global update* function. In a card catalog, the equivalent of global updating can be as elaborate as retyping every card or as simple as filing a new reference or guide card explaining the change.

A second consideration for ongoing authority control work is what to do about changed headings. Subject headings change frequently to reflect changes in language, to make subject headings more consistent with one another, to accommodate new areas of knowledge, or to maintain accuracy (a situation that occurs frequently with place-names). The library needs a way to be aware of and make these changes. Again, a number of choices are available.

A librarian may ask the authority control vendor to retain a copy of the library's authority and bibliographic records. Then, whenever one of the headings changes, the vendor sends a new copy of the record or any associated authority records or both to the library. A variation on this theme is a *notification service*, in which the vendor sends lists of changes to the library and the library makes the changes in-house. A low-tech but more time-consuming method is for the librarian to use the Library of Congress weekly lists (of subject heading changes), the quarterly *Cataloging Service Bulletin*, or other sources available that list the changes, and manually revise authority and associated bibliographic records. Most libraries rely on some combination of options.

Finally, there is the question of the level of detail in authority maintenance. How exhaustive should your authority control be? In theory, a true authority-controlled catalog has an associated authority record for every single access point it contains. Additionally, every cross-reference in every one of those authority records is checked for accuracy and deleted or enhanced as required. It should be obvious that this level of rigor is next to impossible for all libraries to achieve. In 1995, Jennifer Younger proposed that the concept of *utility* be applied to authority control, focusing authority control efforts on names that are most likely to lead to confusion for the patron if they are not controlled.[8] Although Younger was specifically discussing name headings, her concept could apply to the whole of authority work.

A Word about Filing

This chapter focuses mainly on how headings are established for use in the catalog and how they are maintained, not on how the resulting headings should be arranged in the catalog. However, this is a good place to take a look at that matter. Authority files alphabetize their listings, both names and subject headings. This suggests it is an easy matter to find the authorized headings one wants and arrange them in the catalog, but the reality is that alphabetizing is not simple. Problems occur in deciding how to handle initials, digits, abbreviations, and the like. Since 1980, there have been two methods of alphabetizing, embodied in two different tools: the *ALA Filing Rules* and the *Library of Congress Filing Rules*.[9] Both tools share several basic principles. First, headings are filed word-by-word, not letter-by-letter as is commonly done in telephone books, and second, words are filed as they appear, not as they might be spoken; for example, "Dr." is filed as "d, r, period," not as if it were really "doctor." The second principle takes care of abbreviations. A third common principle is that digits are filed as digits, preceding alphabetic characters, and are arranged in increasing numerical value. Here, the commonalities stop. Each tool has its own principles governing how to deal with subject headings consisting of more than one word or more than one part or both.

The ALA rules ignore the punctuation that separates subject headings into parts, such as **United States—History** and **Paintings, American.** Under its rules, both headings would file as if they had no punctuation and were written as United States History and Paintings American. The LC rules recognize different marks of punctuation and file headings differently according to the type of heading or subdivision and how they are encoded in the MARC format. Under LC rules, the two headings would translate into "Main heading = United States; subdivision subfield x = History" and "Inverted main heading = Paintings, American." In the LC rules, a main heading and its subdivisions file before another main heading beginning with the same word or words, and different types of subdivisions, represented by MARC subfields v, x, y, and z, file in the following order: subfield y (period); v and x (form and topical); z (geographic). Inverted headings file before words in direct order; thus, the LC heading **Painting, Yugoslav** files before **Painting knives.** In the ALA rules, however, **Painting knives** would precede **Painting, Yugoslav,** because of ALA's rule to ignore punctuation. The LC rules recognize other marks of punctuation, such as parentheses, name-title headings, and so on, and are provided in the prefatory material in the subject heading list.[10]

Sears List of Subject Headings follows the ALA filing rules. The Library of Congress follows its own rules for its subject headings, both for adult materials and the Annotated Card headings.

Conclusion

Remember, no matter what decisions you make for applying authority control to your catalog, you should keep the needs of your users foremost in mind. Particularly for a children's catalog, expend your efforts first and foremost in those areas that will help children deal with confusing levels of language used to retrieve information. The work you do in the background may make the difference between a frustrated child and a happy one who will see the library and its catalog as a valuable tool he or she can use successfully.

Notes

1. Doris Hargrett Clack, *Authority Control: Principles, Applications, and Instructions* (Chicago: American Library Association, 1990), 2.
2. Robert L. Maxwell, *Maxwell's Guide to Authority Work* (Chicago: American Library Association, 2002), 1.
3. Maxwell, *Maxwell's Guide to Authority Work*, 3.
4. Paul Solomon, "Information Systems for Children: Explorations in Information Access and Interface Usability for an Online Catalog in an Elementary School Library" (PhD diss., University of Maryland, College Park, 1990), abstract in *Digital Dissertations*: AAT 9133166.
5. Frances F. Jacobson, "From Dewey to Mosaic: Considerations in Interface Design for Children," *Internet Research: Electronic Networking Applications and Policy* 5, no. 2 (1995): 68.
6. Pam Sandlian, "Rethinking the Rules," *School Library Journal* (1995): 24.
7. Shuyuan Zhao, "Use-Based Virtual Reorganization of a Library Collection: An Empirical Study," (PhD diss., Rutgers, the State University of New Jersey, New Brunswick, 2000), abstract in *Digital Dissertations*: AAT 9974003.
8. Jennifer A. Younger, "After Cutter: Authority Control in the Twenty-first Century," *Library Resources and Technical Services* 39, no. 2 (April 1995): 133–41.
9. *ALA Filing Rules* (Chicago: American Library Association, 1980); and *Library of Congress Filing Rules*, prepared by John C. Rather and Susan C. Biebel (Washington, DC: Library of Congress, 1980).
10. *Library of Congress Subject Headings*, 26th ed. (Washington, DC: Cataloging Distribution Service, 2003), xvi.

6

Using LC's Children's Headings for Original MARC Cataloging: Why and How

Joanna F. Fountain

One of the most challenging and interesting areas of cataloging is the creation of original machine-readable cataloging records for children's materials. The cataloger must address the needs of multiple audiences while juggling complicated rules, rule interpretations, special guidelines for children's catalogs, classification options, and curriculum-enhancement features. For the school or public librarian who is not a full-time or highly experienced cataloger, this can be a daunting task. Fortunately, many have the opportunity to purchase cataloging records from a variety of sources. Still, the quality of the records available for purchase varies from excellent to erroneous, and children's catalogs—which should be the most helpful—often contain entries that mislead rather than assist younger library users in finding what they seek.

The intent of this chapter is to walk through the guidelines for using the list of subject headings for children's catalogs (LCSH, 2004) compiled by the Library of Congress (LC).[1] The Cataloging and Classification Section (CCS) of the Resources and Technical Services Division (RTSD) of the American Library Association (ALA)—now renamed the Association for Library Collections and Technical Services (ALCTS)—has recommended very similar policies and practices for general use in children's catalogs. These guidelines address the needs of children and youth, librarians, teachers, parents, and others interested in working with young readers and catalog users. Such varied audiences call for several levels and types of information; however, once the principles are understood, catalogers can apply them, knowing they have a sound basis for making the judgments that go into creating useful and usable bibliographic records.

In order to catalog children's materials according to ALA and LC guidelines, you must have access to a particular body of cataloging tools. They include the latest revision of the *Anglo-American Cataloguing Rules* (AACR2) and its amendments, ALA's "Guidelines for Standardized Cataloging for Children" (see chapter 1 in this book), a copy of the *Abridged Dewey Decimal Classification and Relative Index*, applicable Library of Congress rule interpretations, a copy (in any format) of the *Library of Congress Subject Headings* (LCSH), and a copy of the curriculum-enhancement guidelines approved by ALA's MARBI (Committee on Representation in Machine-Readable Form of Bibliographic Information) in June 1993 for use in children's catalogs.[2]

Specific instructions for applying the supplemental heading list in children's catalogs are provided in the first volume of each print edition of LCSH, in the section titled "Annotated Card Program: AC Subject Headings." That section describes LC's policies for subject analysis and application of the supplemental AC list to children's materials in their collection as well as for the valuable Cataloging-in-Publication (CIP) program. The AC list itself provides modifications and exceptions to the main list, but does not replace it. Policies applied to children's books and other library materials at the Library of Congress are spelled out in section D500 of the *Subject Cataloging Manual: General Cataloging Procedures*, titled "Juvenile Materials." Selection for AC program treatment for some materials is based on the stated or presumed audience level of the work *after* the basic description has been written, when members of LC's subject cataloging teams make the initial identification as part of their normal procedures and assign main LC subject headings according to standard subject cataloging policy. If a work is a candidate for treatment by the AC program, the item is routed to the Children's Literature team for their attention. The AC program's scope includes all English-language juvenile publications, regardless of country of publication, and all juvenile publications published in the United States, regardless of the language of publication.

Fiction and nonfiction works are treated differently in the AC program: a nonfiction item is treated as juvenile if it is intended primarily for children and young people through the age of fifteen, or ninth grade. Fiction intended primarily for children and young people *through high school age* is also treated as juvenile. These definitions vary only slightly from ALA Guidelines, which identify the upper limit of juvenile collections more generally as "through junior high level" and state that the application of the Guidelines to high school–level materials is optional.

Once the "juvenile" determination has been made, the Children's Literature team assigns Machine-Readable Cataloging (MARC) codes for fixed-field elements, classifies the work according to instructions in section F615 of the *Subject Cataloging Manual: Classification*, selecting the appropriate LC Classification (LCC) and supplying the E (Easy) and Fic (Fiction) optional classifications from the Dewey Decimal Classification schedules (DDC). These appear in CIP records and on printed cards in brackets; headings from the AC list are supplied, also in brackets. Subject analysis follows instructions in section H1690 of the *Subject Cataloging Manual: Subject Headings*; for example, subdivisions such as —**Juvenile literature,** which are added to standard subject headings, are excluded from the bracketed headings. Until recently, juvenile works—except for those receiving a descriptive contents note—received a brief, noncritical annotation or summary, entered in the Summary note field (MARC field 520).[3] Because notes are occasionally curtailed due to fiscal constraints, it is unlikely that curriculum enhancements—which add to the time required for producing a full juvenile cataloging record—will become part of AC program cataloging in the near future, despite being included in the USMARC code in 1994.

The Children's Literature team generally has complete responsibility for juvenile belles lettres; fictional works are not always assigned any subject headings by the AC program—again because of budget constraints. When they are omitted, the task of assigning subject headings to fiction is left to local librarians, as it is generally agreed such headings are especially useful in children's catalogs. Works of nonfiction do receive a full array of subject headings, with MARC coding, and appropriate classification numbers. When the team completes its work on an item that has been referred to them for juvenile enhancement, the item is sent back to the original subject cataloging team, and unique book numbers (Cutters) are assigned according to guidelines in LC's *Subject Cataloging Manual: Shelflisting.*

Although librarians in other settings usually do not work in teams or route materials to other staff members, aspects of LC's procedures may be useful to emulate. Three general procedures are followed: (1) each item is described; (2) subject headings are added to the record; and (3) the work is classified. Beginning with the title page, or the chief source of information for nonbook materials, the cataloger first drafts the bibliographic description, following AACR2 rules. Codes for level, illustration, and so on are added to the MARC record according to instructions online at http://www.loc.gov/marc, or in the printed MARC documentation and manuals that accompany the automated catalog program being used.

Next, subject headings are added, either from the *Sears List of Subject Headings* or from LCSH. Libraries that use CIP and other LC records in their catalogs will normally use LCSH as their source. (More detailed description of this process is given later in this chapter.) Local modifications or additions, if any, are noted in the local authority file, and care is taken to enter these only in "local" fields of the MARC record. Authority files are then checked to ensure consistency in the form of all names and titles used as main and added entries, including subject added entries.

Finally, call numbers are assigned: first the classification is determined, and then the local Cutter (alphabetizing or other sequencing feature) is added. The shelflist is checked for appropriate placement within the collection, and any other information, such as copy number, will be added at this point.

The remainder of this chapter focuses on the selection and assignment of subject headings for children, with LCSH, including its children's subject list, as the authority. After writing down or mentally noting possible terms to describe what the work is about, the cataloger begins by verifying them in *both* the main list (currently five printed volumes) and the AC list (in the first volume), because by definition the two lists are in conflict. AC headings and subdivisions are exceptions to standard LCSH usage, and there are no references from the main list to the AC (children's) terms. After some practice, the cataloger will frequently guess (or remember) that an alternative term exists in the AC list, and save time by checking that list first. In either sequence, headings from both lists are usually needed. Having verified the existence of a heading, scope notes are read for further instructions. It is wise to review the usage instructions at the beginning of the AC program description occasionally, because they are different enough from standard practice that one may forget the details. This is true even when the online version of LCSH—the LC/NACO Authority File, found at http://authorities.loc.gov—is used as the source of headings and subdivisions. Standard usage for all categories of headings and free-floating subdivisions is presented in detail in the *Subject Cataloging Manual: Subject Headings*. That manual is an essential reference to LC subject cataloging practice.

In many ways LC's instructions are self-explanatory and include representative illustrations. Nevertheless, it helps to study them at some length and read portions of the list to gain a workable level of understanding for their application to the varied audiences the children's cataloger must bear in mind. At least five audiences for cataloging of juvenile works must be considered during the creation or enhancement of bibliographic records: (1) children and young adults; (2) librarians and cataloging support staff; (3) teachers; (4) college students and faculty members; and (5) the public, especially parents.

All subject headings in MARC records are entered in fields with three-numeral tags beginning with a 6, usually referred to generically as 6XX fields. The tag is followed by two additional numeral positions, known as *indicators*. The first is usually blank.[4] The second is a code indicating the source of the heading. A second indicator coded 0 indicates that the heading is from the main LCSH list, and the heading and any subdivisions have been entered according to standard LCSH practice. When a heading or its subdivisions have been taken from the AC list, *or* a "main" heading or subdivision has been assigned according to the guidelines for the AC program, the second indicator is coded 1. (In some automated systems, the absence of that indicator may prevent the printing or display of the summary note found in the 520 field.) You can usually expect a MARC record for a juvenile work to have at least two subject headings: one with a second indicator 0, and one with a second indicator 1. The first is for entries to be filed in standard catalogs; the second is for entries to be filed in children's catalogs, although AC usage has broad appeal and could be considered for use in public catalogs intended for adults as well. A library serving a general user population might retain both types of entry in its catalog if its automated system can index or reference them to resolve conflicts. The children's catalog should not include subject headings with the second indicator 0, however, because the AC program version of the entry provides subject access in the recommended form.

Personal names used as subjects are entered in field 600. Although the Library of Congress does not regularly assign subject headings to works of fiction, librarians are encouraged by ALA Guidelines to do so. This may be done successfully by following LC's AC program guidelines; for example, a story (fiction) about events involving President Abraham Lincoln might have at least the following subject entries:[5]

> 600 _0   Lincoln, Abraham, 1809-1865 ‡v Juvenile fiction
> (for a general catalog)

> 600 _1   Lincoln, Abraham, 1809-1865 ‡v Fiction
> (for a juvenile services catalog)

Nonfictional biographical works (including autobiographies) of individuals have similar headings, but are subdivided differently. In both cases, at least *two* headings are to be entered. The first heading is the individual's name; the second is the "class of persons" with which the biographee is most commonly associated. In some cases, the name of a place, event, or organization with which the person is associated will also be a useful access point.

There are three important differences between standard and AC usage in the assignment of subdivisions. The first is in the application of the subdivision —**Biography**, which is not authorized for use under personal names in standard usage. AC usage for individual biographies of *members of ethnic groups*—including American Indian groups—calls for the free-floating subdivision —**Biography** to be added to the names of individual biographees in children's catalogs. The second major difference is the use of geographic subdivisions in "class of persons" headings in children's catalogs: —**United States** is not used in AC subject entries unless the term is broad or is international in scope, so that the place name is required for accurate interpretation, as with **Folklore—United States**. The opposite is true of standard subdivision practice, in which the geographic subdivision is routinely used for any topic that could reasonably be interpreted as varying from place to place. The same principle applies to standard LCSH headings that include the word *American*, such as **American wit and humor**, or **Short stories, American**; the AC equivalents are **Wit and humor** and **Short stories**. The third important difference in application is in the use of specific and broader entries in the same bibliographic record. In standard LC practice, a broad term is not used *in addition to* a specific term that is encompassed by it. The rule is to be as specific as the content of the work, or *coextensive* with the scope of the work. In AC usage, by contrast, the use of broad and narrower terms is encouraged when their inclusion might provide better access to the work.

The following example illustrates all three differences between standard and AC subject entries; these are headings that would be applied in the case of a juvenile biography of John Chapman (the legendary American apple seed and sprout planter):

600 10   Appleseed, Johnny, 1774-1845 ‡v Juvenile literature

650 _0   Apple growers ‡z United States ‡v Biography ‡v Juvenile literature

600 11   Appleseed, Johnny, 1774-1845

650 _1   Apple growers

650 _1   Horticulturists

In this example, the two standard subject entries—identifiable by the 0 in the second indicator position—have subdivisions that would not be used in AC practice: **—Juvenile literature** and **—United States**. The third AC entry, **Horticulturists**, has no matching standard entry, because it is broader than, and encompasses, the specific term **Apple growers**. Also, the broad term and the narrower term both designate "professions," so the subdivision **—Biography** is not used. By using a second indicator of 1, the cataloger alerts searchers looking at the record that the term is applied according to AC usage, although it is a standard term used with the standard application of a free-floating subdivision.

A different modification of subdivision practice for use in children's catalogs is encountered in headings for adapted versions of works. The following example is for a film version of Anton Chekhov's *The Cherry Orchard*. The title portion of the name-title entry has been modified for AC usage, replacing the original Russian title with the English-language title by which English-speaking readers know the work. Note that no form subdivision is available for use in the AC program as a counterpart for the subdivision **—Juvenile films**. Subject headings for this work would include

> 600 10 Chekhov, Anton Pavlovich, 1860-1904. ‡t Vishnevyi sad ‡v Juvenile films
>
> 600 11 Chekhov, Anton Pavlovich, 1860-1904. ‡t Cherry orchard

In this example, the first indicator 1 represents the form of the surname (single), for filing purposes. The second indicator in a 6XX field, as noted previously, represents the authority for or the source of the subject heading, in this case the AC list.

Works *about other works* or that are adaptations of other works with known authors are always (and only) entered under the name of the author of the original work. This is especially helpful in collocating all the forms, versions, adaptations, editions, and so on of the same work, because the titles proper often vary, forcing such variations away from each other alphabetically in the catalog. Only titles of anonymous works and works that for other reasons have a uniform title as main entry may be accessed in the subject portion of the catalog directly under their titles. Uniform titles used as subjects are entered in MARC field 630. A children's play based on such a work might have such subject entries as

> 630 00 Chanson de Roland. ‡l English ‡v Juvenile drama
>
> 630 01 Chanson de Roland. ‡l English ‡v Drama

In this example, the first indicator 0 represents nonfiling characters in the entry. AACR2 prescribes omission of leading articles in uniform titles, so a zero indicator is used for any uniform title used as a subject or name entry. In addition to uniform titles for individual works, titles of series and collective titles are entered in 630 fields when they are the subject of other works. Note that the AC list does provide the subdivision —**Drama** as an alternative to the standard subdivision —**Juvenile drama**.

Each type of name heading is entered in a different field number. For example, corporate-body names are tagged 610, conference names are in field 611, and geographic or place names in field 651. The most commonly used subject field tag, however, is 650. It is used for topical subjects, including any identifiable topic for fictional works. A children's book about coral snakes will have the following entries:

> 650 _0 Micrurus ‡v Juvenile literature
>
> 650 _1 Coral snakes

For many nonfiction works, no subdivision is required for juvenile subject entries. Yet there are a number of exceptions. Some are listed in the AC list, while others are available as free-floating subdivisions for either standard or AC headings. Others are listed in the AC instructions. For example, all works of juvenile fiction should have a topical entry if possible. The well-known work *Charlotte's Web* might have the following subjects as added entries:

650 _0   Spiders ‡v Juvenile fiction

650 _0   Death and dying ‡v Juvenile fiction

650 _1   Spiders ‡v Fiction

650 _1   Death and dying ‡v Fiction

Many additions and modifications have been made to enhance use of children's materials. Some are modified and noted in the AC list, while others are to be modified by instruction, as seen in the preceding examples. The list includes a number of terms that have been added for the benefit of persons working *with* children and young adults—terms that younger readers might not think to use as access points. For example, the term **Textures**, which is not used in the standard list, would be of interest to a parent or teacher, but not necessarily to young children. Similarly, the subdivision —**Collections** is no longer authorized as a standard LCSH free-floating subdivision; nevertheless, it is still to be used with certain headings in children's catalogs, such as **Storytelling—Collections**, because of its usefulness to librarians and teachers in making selections for young readers.

Teachers and librarians occasionally develop reading lists for bibliotherapy and independent reading on a variety of topics and levels. The special children's headings in the AC list supplement standard headings and make it easier to identify material using terms more familiar to younger readers. **Gas**, for example, replaces the standard LCSH term Natural gas; the term Marriage is modified for AC use, so that it replaces the main-list term **Teenage marriage**.

Children and young adults are considered the ultimate users of the juvenile catalog. For this reason, the greatest part of the AC list consists of substitutions for standard LCSH terms. Each year several of the substituted terms have replaced less commonly used and obsolete terms in the *main* listing of subject headings. As a result, those terms have been removed from the children's heading list and are now considered standard. Their use as standard headings benefits all catalog users without diminishing children's catalogs in any way.

Examples of headings removed from the AC list because they have become standard are **Music camps** (which replaced Camps, Music), **Cave drawings** (which had been spelled with a hyphen in the standard list), and **Roe deer** (which had been substituted for Capreolus). In addition, the name **Coronado, Francisco Vásquez de, 1510-1554** has replaced Vásquez de Coronado, Francisco, 1510-1554 in the Library of Congress's name authority file.

Other examples of substituted terms are combined terms, such as **Actors and actresses, Lost and found possessions**, and **Waiters and waitresses**. Some AC headings replace more than one standard heading without actually combining them. For example, **Babies** replaces both Infants, and Infants (Newborn); and **Lesser**

panda replaces Ailurus fulgens, Red panda, and Wah. **Kings, queens, rulers, etc.** is used in place of *twelve* terms in the main list: Caliphs, Emperors, Monarchs, Pharaohs, Queens, Roman emperors, Royalty, Rulers, Russian empresses, Shahs, Sovereigns, and Sultans!

Popular terms replacing *less* commonly-used terms include **Greed** (used for [UF] Avarice), **Luck** (UF Fortune), and **Menstruation** (UF Menstrual cycle). Similarly, shorter forms of headings sometimes replace longer forms; **Baseball— Fiction** is used instead of Baseball stories, for example, and **Jumping bean** replaces Mexican jumping bean. Occasionally the use of some AC terms seems contradictory, such as **Horror stories**, instead of Horror—Fiction and Horror tales, but on examination those terms are found to be more popular.

Scientific terms are frequently replaced with more popular terms, even though children and youth are not likely to use the popular term to a great extent either; for example, **Livebearers (Fish)** replaces Poeciliidae, and **Isopods** replaces Isopoda. Some terms, however, are more common, such as **Snakes**, used for Serpents, and **Test tube babies**, used for Fertilization in vitro, Human. For older children and youth who are more familiar with the natural world and who may be studying scientific topics, it is recommended that both the popular term *and* the scientific term be used in the bibliographic record as access points. When both terms are used in the same catalog, however, some accommodation to the reference structure will be required; for example, *see also* or RT (related term) references might resolve conflicts.

Both ALA and LC's AC program recommend use of both broad and specific headings as useful access points. Although this practice would be good to apply generally, LC's standard policy for subject-heading assignment has in the past led the way to decreased use of this obvious and helpful aid to catalog users. The AC program does, however, recognize that young people frequently refer to topics in more inclusive groupings than older people might. For example, a child or other person might use the term *space* to refer to any of a number of more specific topics, such as space travel, space exploration, astronomy, the universe, and so on. Whenever such broad terms are available in either the main list or the AC list, they should be used as access points *in addition to* the more specific terms. Some general terms are specified in the AC list to actually replace main headings, such as **Dogs** in place of Puppies, or **Chickens** instead of Chicks.

The AC list provides special treatment for works in non-English languages and bilingual works in languages that have been established in the AC list. Headings follow two patterns: the first is for informational and recreational works in a language, including bilingual works; the second is for works designed for instruction and practice in reading the language, commonly referred to as *readers*. The heading for the first broad grouping follows the pattern **French language materials, Chippewa**

language materials, and so on. This type of heading may in turn be followed by the subdivision —**Bilingual** when necessary. The second pattern is the same term without the word *materials*; this type of heading may be followed by any applicable free-floating subdivision, or by the special AC language subdivision, as **Hebrew language, German language—Collections,** or **Spanish language—Readers.**

In addition to heading modification, a number of subdivisions have special applications. In addition to —**Collections,** mentioned earlier, the following subdivisions are used only in children's catalogs: —**Cartoons and comics,** —**Guides** (use differs in the main list), —**Habits and behaviors,** and —**Wit and humor.** On the other hand, the subdivision —**Illustrations** is not used; instead, the subdivision —**Pictorial works** replaces it in AC usage. Also discussed earlier are the particular AC usage guidelines for the standard subdivision —**Biography,** which has a specific *limitation* in that it may only be used in topical entries under names of ethnic groups (including the older category Indians) and under subject fields in which no specific term designates the profession or contributions of the biographee; for example, it may not be used under **Teachers,** because that term designates a profession.

Headings and free-floating subdivisions in the standard list that begin with the words Children, Children's, or Juvenile are to be used without those words in AC headings; the same is true for headings ending with such phrases as "for children" or "in children." Some examples of the latter are **Strangers,** which replaces Children and strangers, and **Separation anxiety,** used instead of Separation anxiety in children.

In summary, both ALA's Guidelines and the Library of Congress's Annotated Card program are outgrowths of the clear need to modify standard catalog access and arrangement of materials for children's catalogs. Their purpose is to increase the likelihood that younger readers will find what they want and need, in terms they use and understand. Both sets of guidelines outline modifications of terminology and access-point selection that increase that possibility. The result is that the cataloger will write longer, more inclusive bibliographic records, supplying both general and specific levels of vocabulary as subject access points and assigning headings that reflect both adult and children's language use. In headings for the youthful reader, superfluous terms related to youth are omitted, and special subdivisions are added to others to increase their comprehensibility. These guidelines do not foster more or faster cataloging, but are undoubtedly better for the catalog user. We are *still* indebted to Charles Ammi Cutter for his clear statements of our objectives in cataloging, including his admonition that "the convenience of the public is always to be set before the ease of the cataloger."[6] He further took care to point out that both guidelines and thought are required to achieve our purposes, stating, "Cataloging is an art, not a science. No rules can take the place of experience and good judgment, but some of the results of experience may be best indicated by rules."

Notes

1. Library of Congress, Subject Cataloging Division, *Library of Congress Subject Headings* (LCSH), 27th ed. (Washington, DC: Library of Congress, Cataloging Distribution Service, 2004).
2. USMARC revisions for curriculum enhancements published as of 2004.
3. Jane E. Gilchrist, "The Annotated Card Program," in *Cataloging Correctly for Kids: An Introduction to the Tools*, 3rd ed., ed. Sharon Zuiderveld (Chicago: American Library Association, 1998).
4. Blank positions are represented in examples by an underscore.
5. Subfield delimiters are represented in examples by a ‡ (double dagger, or diesis). Note, however, that many printers do not accommodate this character, so this symbol is frequently represented by a $ (dollar mark).
6. Charles A. Cutter, "Rules for a Dictionary Catalog: Selections," in *Foundations of Cataloging: A Sourcebook*, ed. Michael Carpenter and Elaine Svenonius (Littleton, CO: Libraries Unlimited, 1985).

Bibliography

Abridged Dewey Decimal Classification and Relative Index. 14th ed. Dublin, OH: OCLC, 2004.

Anglo-American Cataloguing Rules. 2nd ed., 2002 rev., 2004 update. Chicago: American Library Association, 2002.

"Annotated Card Program: AC Subject Headings." In *Library of Congress Subject Headings* (LCSH). 26th ed. Vol. 1. Washington, DC: Library of Congress, Cataloging Distribution Service, 2003.

Association for Library Collections and Technical Services/CCS Cataloging of Children's Materials Committee. "Guidelines for Standardized Cataloging of Children's Materials." In *Cataloging Correctly for Kids: An Introduction to the Tools.* 3rd ed. Edited by Sharon Zuiderveld. Chicago: American Library Association, 1998. First published in *Top of the News* 40 (Fall 1983): 49–55.

"Cataloging for Children: A Selective Bibliography." In *ALCTS Newsletter* 1, no. 4 (1990): 40–41.

Cutter, Charles A. "Rules for a Dictionary Catalog: Selections." In *Foundations of Cataloging: A Sourcebook*, edited by Michael Carpenter and Elaine Svenonius. Littleton, CO: Libraries Unlimited, 1985.

Dewey Decimal Classification and Relative Index. 22nd ed. Dublin, OH: OCLC (Online Computer Library Center), 2003.

Gilchrist, Jane E. "The Annotated Card Program." *In Cataloging Correctly for Kids: An Introduction to the Tools.* 3rd ed. Edited by Sharon Zuiderveld. Chicago: American Library Association, 1998.

"Juvenile Materials, D500." In *Subject Cataloging Manual: General Cataloging Procedures.* Washington, DC: Library of Congress, Cataloging Distribution Service, 1992.

LC/NACO Authority File [topics, names, titles], http://authorities.loc.gov [always current].

Library of Congress. Network Development and MARC Standards Office. *MARC 21 Format for Bibliographic Data.* Washington, DC: Library of Congress, Cataloging Distribution Service, 1999 [with updates to 2004].

Library of Congress. Subject Cataloging Division. *Library of Congress Classification Schedules, A–Z* (LCC). Washington, DC: Library of Congress, Cataloging Distribution Service. [Dates of the forty-three current editions vary.]

————. *Library of Congress Rule Interpretations.* Washington, DC: Library of Congress, Cataloging Distribution Service, 1989 [with updates through 2002].

————. *Library of Congress Subject Headings* (LCSH). 27th ed. Washington, DC: Library of Congress, Cataloging Distribution Service, 2004.

————. *Subject Cataloging Manual: Classification.* Washington, DC: Library of Congress, Cataloging Distribution Service, 1992 [with 2005 update].

————. *Subject Cataloging Manual: Shelflisting.* Washington, DC: Library of Congress, Cataloging Distribution Service, 1987.

————. *Subject Cataloging Manual: Subject Headings* (SCM:SH). 5th ed. Washington, DC: Library of Congress, Cataloging Distribution Service, 1996 [with updates through 2004].

7

Sears List of Subject Headings

Joseph Miller

Two sources of subject headings exist for cataloging children's materials. The first is *Library of Congress Subject Headings* (LCSH) together with the modified list of Annotated Card (AC) headings used by the Library of Congress for children's materials only. The AC headings are found in the front of the first volume of the print edition of LCSH and also in electronic form. The second source is the *Sears List of Subject Headings* (Sears). These two lists are subject authority environments entirely complete within themselves, and a library will use either one or the other, but never both.

Librarians felt the need for two authority lists early in the twentieth century. In 1923, when the Sears List first appeared, the Library of Congress's *Subject Headings Used in the Dictionary Catalogs of the Library of Congress* and the American Library Association's *List of Subject Headings for Use in Dictionary Catalogs* already existed. Then as now, the Library of Congress tailored its subject headings to its own needs, which are those of a very large research library and quite different from the cataloging needs of small libraries. It was with this difference in mind that Minnie Earl Sears consulted the catalogs of a number of small libraries that she considered well cataloged and put together a list entitled *List of Subject Headings for Small Libraries*. Beginning with the sixth edition (1950), the List was given her name and has since been known as the Sears List. The Sears List has never been intended exclusively for cataloging children's materials. It is meant to be used in any kind of small library.

The original plan of the Sears List was to remain as close as possible to the usage of the Library of Congress to make it possible for a library to change from Sears headings to LC headings when it grew larger. Since that time, however, the two worlds of Sears and LCSH have grown more distinct and separate, although they still share important common ground. Both are alphabetical subject lists, not true thesauri. Both are based on the principle of precoordinated subject strings with the use of subdivisions rather than discrete terms to be coordinated by the end user. Both are based on literary warrant and make no attempt to establish headings before there are library materials requiring such headings. And both are devised for the implementation of Cutter's Rule for the cataloging of materials to the greatest possible level of specificity.

Although Sears continues to maintain conformity to the usage of the Library of Congress to a considerable degree, there are nonetheless a number of differences between the two lists. In general, Sears has fewer technical terms, preferring the common names of things over the scientific names. There are other differences as well. Beginning with the fifteenth edition (1994), Sears converted all its remaining inverted headings to the uninverted form, while LC maintains a combination of inverted and uninverted headings. Currently, for example, **Education, Elementary** in LC is **Elementary education** in Sears. In some cases the vocabulary itself differs. For example, in the seventeenth edition (2000), Sears canceled all its headings for **Indians of North America, Indians of Mexico, Indians of South America,** and so on in favor of the single heading **Native Americans,** which may be subdivided geographically by continent, country, region, state, and so on. Sears also differs from LC in its use of subdivisions. Sears allows for direct geographic subdivisions rather than indirect. For example, Sears would have **Bridges—Chicago (Ill.),** where LC would have **Bridges—Illinois—Chicago.** These are all differences that must be kept in mind when LC MARC records or LC Cataloging-in-Publication (CIP) data are being adapted for a catalog using Sears headings.

The greatest difference between the two lists is that the Library of Congress establishes in its list every heading that has been used in its catalog, with the exception of subject strings involving standard geographic or free-floating subdivisions. The Sears List aims instead to be a pattern or model for the creation of headings as needed. As a result it is less detailed and complete than LCSH but also much smaller, more flexible, and less expensive. In Sears, for example, at the heading for **Animals** there is a general reference note authorizing the creation of headings for types of animals and species of animals as needed. Likewise at **Dogs,** there is a provision for creating headings for types of dogs and breeds of dogs as needed. The cataloger is not encouraged to put a book on collies under **Dogs,** but in very small libraries that is always an option. Even when there is no general reference note in Sears providing for kinds of things and names of specific things under the heading for the thing, it is implied by the nature of the system that those headings can always be created. The Sears List also contains an abundance of general references giving instructions on the application of topical and form subdivisions. An example of a very complete general reference, which draws the distinction between two similar but not interchangeable subdivisions, can be found under the heading **Ethics:** SA [See also] types of ethics, e.g. Business ethics; ethics of particular religions, e.g. Christian ethics; names of individual persons, classes of persons, types of professions, and types of professional personnel with the subdivision Ethics, e.g. Librarians—Ethics; Shakespeare, William, 1564-1616—Ethics; etc., and subjects with the subdivision Ethical aspects, e.g. Birth control—Ethical aspects {to be added as needed}.

For every subdivision provided for in the Sears List there is a general reference with specific instructions on its use. Subdivisions that are not also subject headings, such as *Ethical aspects*, also have an entry with a general reference in their alphabetical place in the List. There is also a complete list of the subdivisions provided for in the Sears List in the front matter of the printed volume. Other subdivisions can be established by the cataloger, if needed.

Both LCSH and Sears are now printed in a thesaurus-like display with broader, narrower, and related terms in the lists indicated with the labels BT, NT, and RT. Every heading in the Sears List is also assigned one or more numbers from the abridged edition of the *Dewey Decimal Classification* (DDC). These DDC numbers in Sears are meant only as pointers to the place or places in the Classification where materials on a particular subject are most likely to be dealt with, not as a guide for classifying any individual item. The numbers should not be assigned to books or other materials without first consulting the schedules and tables of the DDC itself. Furthermore, because changes are made in the DDC periodically, the numbers in Sears can be out of date in certain parts of the Classification. The Sears headings can also be found as access vocabulary in OCLC's *Abridged WebDewey* product.

One obvious advantage of the Sears List over LCSH for a small library is its size. The entire list is contained in one handy volume, while LCSH is now published in five very large volumes, with cross-references spanning the set. The Sears List is correspondingly cheaper. The eighteenth edition of Sears sells for $105, while the twenty-seventh edition of LCSH is $295. A new edition of the Sears List is published every three years, while a new edition of LCSH appears every year. This difference again makes Sears less expensive, but it can pose a problem for libraries with a lot of material on very new topics. Sears produces an updated tape version annually, but it is currently available only to users with mainframe computers, mostly vendors. A web-based version of the Sears List aimed at catalogers in small libraries is in development.

When a need arises for new headings between editions of Sears, librarians can always use headings from the CIP or LC MARC records or from other cataloging and indexing sources by adapting them as necessary. Those Sears-compatible headings should also be incorporated into the library's subject authority file by attaching them to the appropriate broader term from Sears and by establishing cross-references to any narrower or related terms already used in the catalog.

In the era of MARC records and cooperative cataloging, libraries are sometimes under pressure to switch from Sears headings to LC headings. This is a decision that every library must make for itself, based on the perceived advantages and disadvantages of the two subject heading systems. Ideally, that decision is made by a librarian with the interests of the users in mind rather than by an administrator who knows nothing about cataloging. It is not necessary to abandon Sears headings in order to use MARC records. The MARC 21 format provides fully for using Sears headings in the 650 field with the value 7 in the second indicator position and the word *sears* in subfield 2. In the OCLC MARC format, Sears headings are identified by the value 8 in the second indicator position without a subfield 2. Most vendors are able to supply MARC records with Sears headings.

The "Principles of the Sears List of Subject Headings," found in the front of every edition, is a substantial introduction both to the Sears List and to the practice of subject cataloging in general. It has been expanded in the eighteenth edition to provide guidance in assigning topical and geographic headings to individual works of fiction, drama, and poetry. This guidance is contained in nine rules or suggestions that vary in significant ways from the practice of many catalogers. For example, Sears recommends that if both a topical subject and a geographic location are central to a work, they should be expressed separately rather than as a subject string. A novel about horse racing in Florida in which both the topic and the setting are central, for example, should be given the subjects **Horse racing—Fiction** and **Florida—Fiction**. A person looking for novels set in Florida may want this book and might not find it when **—Florida** is appended to another subject.

The same principles of subject analysis are as applicable to Sears as to other subject heading lists, but the shortness and simplicity of the Sears List make it especially practical for small libraries and libraries devoted primarily to children's materials.

Bibliography

Chan, Lois Mai, Phyllis A. Richmond, and Elaine Svenonius, eds. *Theory of Subject Analysis: A Sourcebook.* 2nd ed. Littleton, CO: Libraries Unlimited, 1990.

Cutter, Charles A. *Rules for a Dictionary Catalog.* 4th ed. Washington, DC: U.S. Government Printing Office, 1904.

Ferl, Terry Ellen, and Larry Millsap. *Subject Cataloging: A How-to-Do-It Workbook.* New York: Neal-Schuman, 1991.

Foskett, A. C. *The Subject Approach to Information.* 5th ed. London: The Library Association, 1996.

Intner, Sheila S., and Jean Weihs. *Standard Cataloging for School and Public Libraries.* 3rd ed. Englewood, CO: Libraries Unlimited, 2001.

Rowley, Jennifer. *Organizing Knowledge: An Introduction to Information Retrieval.* Brookfield, VT: Ashgate, 1992.

Sears List of Subject Headings. 18th ed. Edited by Joseph Miller with the assistance of Joan Goodsell. New York: H. W. Wilson, 2004.

Sears List of Subject Headings: Canadian Companion. 6th ed. Edited by Lynne Lighthall. New York: H. W. Wilson, 2001.

Taylor, Arlene G. *The Organization of Information.* 2nd ed. Westport, CT: Libraries Unlimited, 2003.

―――. *Wynar's Introduction to Cataloging and Classification.* 9th ed. Englewood, CO: Libraries Unlimited, 2000.

8

Sources for Dewey Numbers

Gregory R. New

The biggest single source for Dewey Decimal Classification numbers for American libraries since 1930 has been the Library of Congress (LC).[1] In the early days, the source was called "DC on LC," that is, Dewey Classification numbers on Library of Congress cards. For thirty-five years, Dewey numbers were added to records for twenty thousand to thirty thousand titles per year. From 1966 to 1975 there was a spurt of growth, and each year since then, LC has supplied Dewey numbers for more than one hundred thousand titles per year. These numbers appear in the MARC records available via Internet FTP pickup and on the Web. These records are the original source of cataloging information that many libraries obtain when they buy cards or electronic cataloging from vendors, or download electronic records from bibliographic utilities.

Other libraries also contribute Dewey numbers to bibliographic utilities, however. Thus, one may not always be able to tell who did the original classification that helps readers find their way in book collections. Undoubtedly, however, many of the Dewey numbers in American libraries were originally assigned at the Library of Congress.

The Dewey Family: History and Background

Several large institutions cooperate to maintain the Dewey Decimal Classification (DDC). These include parts of the Library of Congress, OCLC (Online Computer Library Center), and the American Library Association (ALA). Most of the staff work is done in the Decimal Classification Division at the Library of Congress. The application of the Classification, currently running about one hundred thousand

and indexing sources by adapting them as necessary. Those Sears-compatible headings should also be incorporated into the library's subject authority file by attaching them to the appropriate broader term from Sears and by establishing cross-references to any narrower or related terms already used in the catalog.

In the era of MARC records and cooperative cataloging, libraries are sometimes under pressure to switch from Sears headings to LC headings. This is a decision that every library must make for itself, based on the perceived advantages and disadvantages of the two subject heading systems. Ideally, that decision is made by a librarian with the interests of the users in mind rather than by an administrator who knows nothing about cataloging. It is not necessary to abandon Sears headings in order to use MARC records. The MARC 21 format provides fully for using Sears headings in the 650 field with the value 7 in the second indicator position and the word *sears* in subfield 2. In the OCLC MARC format, Sears headings are identified by the value 8 in the second indicator position without a subfield 2. Most vendors are able to supply MARC records with Sears headings.

The "Principles of the Sears List of Subject Headings," found in the front of every edition, is a substantial introduction both to the Sears List and to the practice of subject cataloging in general. It has been expanded in the eighteenth edition to provide guidance in assigning topical and geographic headings to individual works of fiction, drama, and poetry. This guidance is contained in nine rules or suggestions that vary in significant ways from the practice of many catalogers. For example, Sears recommends that if both a topical subject and a geographic location are central to a work, they should be expressed separately rather than as a subject string. A novel about horse racing in Florida in which both the topic and the setting are central, for example, should be given the subjects **Horse racing—Fiction** and **Florida—Fiction.** A person looking for novels set in Florida may want this book and might not find it when **—Florida** is appended to another subject.

The same principles of subject analysis are as applicable to Sears as to other subject heading lists, but the shortness and simplicity of the Sears List make it especially practical for small libraries and libraries devoted primarily to children's materials.

Bibliography

Chan, Lois Mai, Phyllis A. Richmond, and Elaine Svenonius, eds. *Theory of Subject Analysis: A Sourcebook.* 2nd ed. Littleton, CO: Libraries Unlimited, 1990.

Cutter, Charles A. *Rules for a Dictionary Catalog.* 4th ed. Washington, DC: U.S. Government Printing Office, 1904.

Ferl, Terry Ellen, and Larry Millsap. *Subject Cataloging: A How-to-Do-It Workbook.* New York: Neal-Schuman, 1991.

Foskett, A. C. *The Subject Approach to Information.* 5th ed. London: The Library Association, 1996.

Intner, Sheila S., and Jean Weihs. *Standard Cataloging for School and Public Libraries.* 3rd ed. Englewood, CO: Libraries Unlimited, 2001.

Rowley, Jennifer. *Organizing Knowledge: An Introduction to Information Retrieval.* Brookfield, VT: Ashgate, 1992.

Sears List of Subject Headings. 18th ed. Edited by Joseph Miller with the assistance of Joan Goodsell. New York: H. W. Wilson, 2004.

Sears List of Subject Headings: Canadian Companion. 6th ed. Edited by Lynne Lighthall. New York: H. W. Wilson, 2001.

Taylor, Arlene G. *The Organization of Information.* 2nd ed. Westport, CT: Libraries Unlimited, 2003.

———. *Wynar's Introduction to Cataloging and Classification.* 9th ed. Englewood, CO: Libraries Unlimited, 2000.

titles per year, is supported by appropriated funds as is most work of federal agencies. The editing, however, is done under an agreement with OCLC, which holds the Dewey copyright. OCLC obtains the funds that support the editing largely from the sale of full and abridged editions of the Classification in print and electronic versions and related publications such as *Dewey Decimal Classification: Principles and Application; Dewey Decimal Classification: 200 Religion Class; People, Places and Things: A List of Popular Library of Congress Subject Headings with Dewey Numbers;* and *Subject Headings for Children: A List of Subject Headings Used by the Library of Congress with Dewey Numbers Added.*[2]

The formal DDC connection with OCLC began in 1988 when OCLC acquired Forest Press, then the publisher of DDC, from the Lake Placid Club Educational Foundation. The name was first used in 1911, when Melvil Dewey gave Edition 7 of his Classification the Forest Press imprint; OCLC retired the Forest Press imprint in 2002. The DDC association with LC began in 1923, when its editorial offices moved to LC. That was seven years before LC began adding Dewey numbers to LC records. The link between DDC and LC provides a convenient editorial environment for developing successive editions of the Classification.

Since 1988, OCLC's role has enabled the Classification to become an integral part of an increasingly sophisticated electronic world. OCLC Research played a major role in developing electronic versions of the DDC. *Electronic Dewey*, a DOS version of the DDC, became available in 1993, and *Dewey for Windows*, a Microsoft Windows–based CD-ROM version of the DDC, was issued annually from 1996 through 2001. *WebDewey* and *Abridged WebDewey*, web-based versions of the current editions of the DDC, are available by subscription from OCLC.

The American Library Association officially came into the picture in 1953, when the Decimal Classification Committee was reconstituted as the DC Editorial Policy Committee (EPC). Of its ten members, four are nominated by ALA; of these, one is designated the official ALA representative. Four other members are selected directly by OCLC: one represents Library and Archives Canada, another the Australian Committee on Cataloguing, and a third represents the Sabinet Online Standards Committee in South Africa. The ninth member represents the Chartered Institute of Library and Information Professionals (CILIP, formerly The [British] Library Association), and the tenth is the associate librarian for library services, Library of Congress.

When a large or difficult revision is on the drawing boards, EPC approaches the Subject Analysis Committee (SAC) of the Cataloging and Classification Section of the Association for Library Collections and Technical Services to appoint a review subcommittee for that schedule. (SAC subcommittees reviewed the revised versions of mathematics, religion, and sociology schedules for the current Edition 22.)

Editors also approach other ALA-related groups on matters on which they have expertise, for example, the Committee on Cataloging: Asian and African Materials. Editors consult with the Cataloging of Children's Materials Committee and the Cataloging Needs of Public Libraries Committee of ALA on matters affecting their respective constituencies, such as what kinds of material and what languages should be given priority in classification. The editors also consult with groups outside ALA, such as the Special Libraries Association.

The EPC is symbolic of the international reach of the Dewey family—the United Kingdom representative keeps the editors in close touch with the CILIP's Dewey Decimal Classification Committee, a group that reviews every draft schedule the editors send to EPC.

In addition to seeking outside review of proposed revisions, EPC seeks libraries to test the more important draft revisions before voting on accepting them. For Edition 22, favorable reports from outside testers were received for revisions in 004–006 (Data processing, Computer science); 200 (Religion); 301–307 (Sociology and anthropology); 341 (International law); and 510 (Mathematics).

Besides those who contribute to the English-language standard editions, three ad hoc groups are organized to translate Dewey. Each group includes an authoritative body, such as a national library, national library association, or national bibliography, to head the translation and provide a mechanism to obtain consensus within a nation or a family of nations on adapting the content to the needs of a given language and culture; a funding source that can be confident its investment will bear fruit; and a team of qualified translators.

Editing the Classification

The editorial staff includes the editor in chief and four assistant editors. Three assistant editors are based at LC. They may confer with the LC-based editors on problems in the areas they edit. The fourth assistant editor is based at OCLC headquarters in Dublin, Ohio, where he is also the Dewey editorial liaison to OCLC development and research staff. In addition to their other duties, all editors answer classification questions from outside the division, thus remaining connected to the world that the Classification serves. In fact, the editors are often alerted to the need for small revisions and clarifications by the questions they receive.

When we move toward a new edition, not long after the previous edition is published, the assistant editors begin preparing drafts of schedules designated for greater and lesser revision. As each draft is prepared, the other editors carefully review it. For schedules undergoing greater revision, successive rounds of drafts and reviews usually take place. Finished drafts eventually are prepared as "exhibits" for EPC. The Committee meets at least once a year for a two- or three-day session or teleconference to review the drafts. Schedules with relatively minor revisions are usually approved at these meetings, subject to various suggestions. The approval consists of a recommendation that the revised schedule be published in the next edition.

For a drastic revision, EPC will usually recommend that the schedule be sent out for review. SAC is called upon to appoint a review subcommittee. Other committees, associations, and individual experts may also be approached. The review process often leads to further drafts, and the whole process usually takes about two years. If the reviews are favorable, chances are greater the revision will be approved when the EPC next considers it.

Sometimes the reviews are not favorable, and the proposed revision must go back for more work, often being recast in the process. The revisions of Education, Life sciences, and Public administration that appeared in Edition 21 went through two or more rounds of reviews. The Life sciences revision was under consideration for twenty-four years before it was finally approved. When doing a major revision, we proceed with care. The revisions proposed for Edition 22 were limited in scope, and all were ultimately approved after improvements and adjustments were made.

The Products

The products currently of greatest interest to libraries for children are *Abridged Dewey Decimal Classification and Relative Index*, Edition 14—the latest printed abridged edition—published in 2004, and *Abridged WebDewey*, an updated electronic version of the abridged Edition 14. Edition 14 is a one-volume condensation of the four-volume full edition, designed for collections with fewer than twenty thousand volumes. Sometimes large public libraries that use the full edition for their main collection use the abridged edition for the children's collection.

Abridged WebDewey is an easy-to-use browser interface that allows users to search efficiently and navigate intuitively; this is especially helpful because many relative index terms are not available in the printed version. Also, Dewey editors have mapped thousands of *Library of Congress Subject Headings* (LCSH) to Dewey numbers, including many from *Subject Headings for Children*. These intellectually mapped LCSH terms are linked to LC subject authority records. Finally, *Abridged WebDewey* includes subject headings from the eighteenth edition of *Sears List of Subject Headings* that have also been mapped to Dewey numbers.

Abridged WebDewey is updated quarterly to incorporate the latest changes to the Classification, new LCSH mappings, index terms, and built numbers. An annotation capability allows a cataloger to add his or her own notes to the local copy of *Abridged WebDewey* to reflect local classification practices. The Dewey website at

OCLC has downloadable Cutter and Cutter-Sanborn four-figure tables that can be used with *Abridged WebDewey* in libraries that require unique call numbers for their holdings.

Classifying Library Material

The Decimal Classification Division (DCD) at LC currently has nine full-time classifiers, who classify an average of more than ten thousand titles each per year. In addition to the full-timers, the chief of DCD, the team leader, and the automated operations coordinator do a significant amount of classifying.

The full-time people are called Decimal Classification specialists. They are assigned broad, overlapping subject specialties. For example, two share responsibility for Science and Technology (500 and 600). One concentrates on Languages and Literature (400 and 800), another on History (900), and a third covers both of these areas as needed. In addition, each classifier has backup specialties so that all fields are covered regardless of the number of absentees. The chief, team leader, and automated operations coordinator also have their subject specialties. The classifiers work very much as a team in a relaxed atmosphere, consult with each other and the editors on classification problems, and pitch in to maintain an even work flow. The classifiers are also ready, as time permits, to entertain questions from users on application and interpretation of the Classification.

The staff assign Dewey numbers to about two-thirds of the full cataloging records distributed by LC, but some material never goes to the DCD office, such as the Cyrillic-alphabet material. When material comes to DCD, we operate on a five-day turnaround—we must send on anything that we cannot classify within a week of receiving it. When the work flow is light, DCD classifies all material for which Dewey numbers appear to be useful. When the work flow is heavy, however, DCD must send on some lower priority material without Dewey numbers.

The situation requires a good sense of priorities. DCD always classifies the Cataloging-in-Publication records and usually completes them on a one-day turnaround. DCD also classifies most American and British trade publications as well as reference works in the major Western European languages. It must sometimes send on other material, but tries to classify as much as possible. Good judgment of the staff about library needs serves as a kind of regulator. Although children's libraries are not an explicit focus of the Division's work, about 10 percent of the one hundred thousand Dewey numbers DCD adds to LC records each year are for children's materials. This number generally includes the books that children's collections most often need to have classified, and confines the gaps mostly to areas where they least need help.

The classifiers work from the latest full edition and produce full edition numbers. Users derive abridged numbers by interpreting the segmentation that appears in the Dewey numbers on bibliographic records produced by LC in MARC field 082. The first segmentation mark can represent either the end of the abridged number or the beginning of a standard subdivision. If the first segmentation mark shows the beginning of a standard subdivision, the second one (if any) shows the end of the abridged standard subdivision.

If your library uses standard subdivisions, check whether the second segment comes from the abridged edition Table 1 Standard Subdivisions. If so, use the second segment; otherwise, do not. If your library does not use standard subdivisions, use only the first segment of the LC-supplied numbers. When your library uses a vendor to catalog books, the vendor interprets the segmentation for you.

Because classifiers in DCD use the full edition as soon as it comes out, there is a short period when you get abridged numbers from an edition that has yet to be published. If you find an odd-looking abridged number during that interval, your best bet is to accept it on faith. That bet is especially good if the mystery number looks like a good place for the material. For example, if you find the number 624.2 being given for Bridges instead of 624, figure that the number has been expanded. What about a hotel directory of the United States in 917.306 instead of in 647.9473? Maybe someone decided it was logical to place facilities for travel next door to the travel numbers. The validity of the mystery numbers can be confirmed by checking "New Features" of the full edition on the Dewey website: http://www.oclc.org/dewey/.

Comparable Dewey numbers are available from other national sources of centralized cataloging copy, such as the British Library in *British National Bibliography* and Library and Archives Canada in *Canadiana*, Canada's national bibliography. When the centralized cataloging is part of a CIP program, the numbers appear in the publications themselves, usually on the back of the title page. In addition, member libraries of electronic union catalogs maintained by bibliographic utilities such as OCLC and RLIN (Research Libraries Information Network) often contribute cataloging copy that includes a Dewey number. Vendors that supply electronic records or cards to individual libraries usually copy from existing sources but do original cataloging when necessary.

When a library is considering a Dewey number found in a bibliographic utility, the MARC coding of the classification number field is a useful aid in evaluating the number. Standard practice is for the number to be in the 082 field. A data element called the *second indicator* (Source of call number) must be checked to determine whether LC or another library supplied the number. If supplied by LC, the second indicator is set to 0; if supplied by another library, the second indicator is set to 4.

Although an outside library number is often a good one, it may reflect practices and options that differ from those adopted by LC classifiers. Also, classifiers in some outside libraries might not be as well trained as classifiers at LC. Thus, numbers with a second indicator 4 should be checked if possible. Normally, numbers assigned by LC can be accepted, provided they conform to the accepting library's own practices and options. For example, a children's collection classed by the abridged edition will need only one or two segments of a three-segment number.

OCLC uses special field 092 (Locally assigned Dewey call number) for Dewey numbers supplied by its member libraries. National agencies that generally conform to LC practice use the 082 field. Other libraries may use either the 092 field or the 082 field with the second indicator set to 4.

Recently, LC has begun to use copy cataloging, which involves starting with an outside library's Dewey number if one appears in the 082 field with valid information in subfield 2 showing which edition the number came from. If the number is verified or corrected by the Decimal Classification Division or one of the classifiers trained by the division, the second indicator is set to 0, the same as if the number were originally assigned by LC. Otherwise, the copied number remains set to 4. Once LC has adapted the records, they appear as Library of Congress MARC records available via FTP pickup or directly downloadable via the Web. Only the second indicator tells whether the Dewey number has been verified (value 0) or simply copied without review (value 4).

In summary, an impressive supply of Dewey numbers is available for works added to children's collections. About ten thousand per year appear in the one hundred thousand records that come from the Library of Congress with Dewey numbers each year, but utilities, vendors, and other libraries also make substantial contributions.

Notes

1. DDC, Dewey, Dewey Decimal Classification, WebDewey, and WorldCat are registered trademarks of OCLC (Online Computer Library Center).
2. Lois Mai Chan and Joan S. Mitchell, *Dewey Decimal Classification: Principles and Application*, 3rd ed. (Dublin, OH: OCLC Online Computer Library Center, 2003); Melvil Dewey, *Dewey Decimal Classification: 200 Religion Class*, devised by Melvil Dewey; edited by Joan S. Mitchell et al. (Dublin OH: OCLC Online Computer Library Center, 2004); *People, Places and Things: A List of Popular Library of Congress Subject Headings with Dewey Numbers* (Dublin, OH: OCLC Forest Press, 2001); and *Subject Headings for Children: A List of Subject Headings Used by the Library of Congress with Dewey Numbers Added*, 2nd ed., edited by Lois Winkel (Albany, NY: OCLC Forest Press, 1998).

9

Cataloging Nonbook Materials

Sheila S. Intner

Materials intended for children's education, information, and recreation are issued in a great variety of physical formats, including books, maps, recordings of many kinds, pictures, games, printed music, electronic forms, and many more, and libraries and media centers catering to children have a long tradition in collecting them. Since 1978, when the second edition of the *Anglo-American Cataloguing Rules* was first issued, catalogers have been able to integrate the cataloging of all physical formats into one work flow and display the results in the same catalog. The term *cataloging standards* now applies to all formats in which library materials appear, from handwritten manuscripts and printed books to Internet websites and online games.

Following a policy of having one catalog for materials in all formats is recommended. From the library's perspective, it enables staff members with the greatest expertise in cataloging to do it all, thus ensuring the best possible results, and it gives all the materials the library buys equal opportunities to be selected and used. From children's perspective, such a policy enables them to look something up in the catalog and see all available editions of a desired work, or all materials a library or media center has on a desired subject or by a particular author, regardless of format. A young searcher may not have any particular type of material in mind, but be open to using any of them. Having one integrated catalog makes such searches possible; at the same time, if the catalog is computerized, as most are in the twenty-first century, it does not prevent a user from limiting the searches to a single medium, if that is what he or she prefers. Creating separate catalogs for nonbook formats, on the other hand, prevents doing integrated searches and forces a child to do multiple searches to see "everything the library has" so he or she can make a choice from the entire range of possibilities.

Integrating the catalog means using the same rules and tools for all materials. These processes are outlined in the following paragraphs.

Descriptive Cataloging

For descriptive cataloging, integrated cataloging means using the current edition of the *Anglo-American Cataloguing Rules* (AACR2).[1] In addition to its first chapter of general rules for describing all materials, AACR2 has chapters to be applied to specific format groups, including maps and other cartographic materials (chapter 3), manuscripts (chapter 4), printed music (chapter 5), recorded music (chapter 6), motion pictures and videorecordings (chapter 7), graphics (chapter 8), electronic resources (chapter 9), three-dimensional materials (chapter 10), microforms (chapter 11), and continuing resources, such as magazines and newspapers (chapter 12).

Physical format is indicated in three places in a bibliographic description: immediately after the main title (area 1); in the descriptive area pertaining to physical description (area 5); and in notes giving additional details about the physical description (area 7). The first indication of format, following the main title, gives a searcher an early warning of an item's physical format. It is called the *general material designation*, or GMD. GMDs are taken from lists in AACR2 and consist of a word or brief phrase indicating a generic medium.[2] They are given in the catalog record in lowercase letters in singular form enclosed in square brackets, because they are supplied by the cataloger, not transcribed directly from the item being cataloged. Following are examples of GMDs for four fictitious nonbook titles:

> Mother Goose [videorecording] : in words & pictures / retold by Jean Doe
>
> Für Elise [music] / Ludwig van Beethoven
>
> Für Elise [sound recording] / Ludwig van Beethoven
>
> The nine Beethoven symphonies [electronic resource]

The next indication of format provides more precise information for the searcher, naming the physical format specifically as part of the extent of the item, while the third indication gives even finer details, as shown in the following catalog records for the same fictitious titles:

```
Mother Goose [videorecording] : in words & pictures /
retold by Jean Doe. — Anniversary ed. — New York : Noname
Distributors, 2004.
    1 videocassette (59 min.) : sd., col. ; ½ in.
    VHS
```

Für Elise [music] / Ludwig van Beethoven. — London :
Allsongs, 2004.
    1 piano score (3 p.) ; 28 cm. + 1 picture.
    Reproduction of original score folded in pocket inside
front cover.

Für Elise [sound recording] / Ludwig van Beethoven. —
Berlin : Recsound, 2004.
    1 sound disc (12 min.) : digital, quad. ; 4¾ in.
    Compact disc.

The nine Beethoven symphonies [electronic resource]. Chicago
: Classical Sounds Online, 2004.
    [No physical description is given because this is a remote access file.]
    Includes images of Beethoven and his living quarters,
pianos, scores, and related documents from the Bonn Archives.

When the bibliographic description is completed, descriptive headings are made for authors, composers, artists, performers, and others responsible for creating a nonbook item; its title and title variants found in or on the item and given in the catalog record; and any series to which the title belongs. These are assigned by applying the rules in part 2 of AACR2 exactly as it is done for books.

Subject Analysis

To maintain an integrated catalog, the same tools from which subject headings and classification numbers are chosen for books are used for the nonbook materials. For the majority of libraries and media centers, this means taking subject headings from either *Sears List of Subject Headings* or *Library of Congress Subject Headings* (see chapters 6 and 7 of this book for additional information on how this is done) and taking classification numbers from either the Dewey Decimal or Library of Congress classifications (see chapter 8 for additional information on how this is done for Dewey; Library of Congress Classification is not covered in this book). If a library uses subject authorities or classification systems or both other than these, they are applied to the nonbook materials as well as to the books.

A distinction is made between the subject matter covered by a nonbook item and its physical aspects. In the past, catalogers treated the physical formats of nonbook materials as though they were the subjects of the items, assigning authorized subject headings such as **Music** or **Video recordings** in addition to, or even in place of, authorized topical headings reflecting the content of the materials. Although headings reflecting physical formats and literary genres are useful, they are not intended to supersede applicable topical subject headings. For example, a videorecording of

E. B. White's *Charlotte's Web* might receive a subject heading for spiders as well as one indicating it is an animated film and another that it is a videorecording. The heading for spiders represents its content—what the video is *about*. The headings for animated films and videorecordings represent aspects of its form—what the video *is*.

Similarly, classification numbers should be assigned to reflect the principal subject of a nonbook item. Its physical format can be included in a full call number by use of a collection prefix, or a format suffix, if that is desired. It is more likely that a student browser will seek nonfiction nonbook materials by their topics than by other access points, although teachers and parents may seek materials by physical format. To accommodate both needs, the library or media center will want to have an online catalog with programming that permits limiting searches by physical format. With this capability, a search for videos about pets or images of London can be retrieved without also retrieving all the books, games, maps, electronic resources, and so on that are also about those subjects.

Although there are differences of opinion about the best way to classify fiction nonbook materials, such as by author or title instead of literature numbers, the best practice locally is to classify nonbook fiction the same way fiction in books is classified.

Generally, classification determines the placement of materials on library shelves, whether for books or nonbook materials. Libraries have four choices about shelving book and nonbook materials: (1) integrate them all into one classification sequence; (2) separate materials by physical format, but follow the same classification sequence for each one (this requires a collection prefix before or above the classification numbers or letters); (3) separate books from nonbook materials, but combine all the nonbook formats and follow the classification sequence in both areas; and (4) integrate some nonbook formats with the books and treat other formats separately or in different combinations, following the classification sequence in each area.[3] The key feature in shelving is to take advantage of the classification sequence for shelf placement, no matter how the parts of each individual collection are deployed. The result will be more satisfying for browsers and reflect the subject matter of the materials more effectively.

MARC Coding

MARC 21, the standard computer markup language for bibliographic data, has been an integrated system for decades, although it once had separate MARC formats for several physical formats, including books, serials, maps, music, and films. Although average catalog records representing nonbook materials are, typically, somewhat longer than those representing books, MARC has been designed with appropriate fields to code the needed data. The additional length of nonbook catalog records is attributable mainly to the increasing number of people, corporate bodies, or both who are responsible for the content, producing more added entries; and the presence of more and longer notes, including system requirements (MARC tag 538), summaries (MARC tag 520), and audience notes, such as reading grade level (MARC tag 521). The greater complexity of some nonbook formats is reflected in additional coded data in several control fields (MARC tags 006, 007, and 008) as well as in the eye-readable portions of the catalog record.

Other Considerations

Catalogers who handle all types of materials in all physical formats need to know current formats and keep up to date as formats evolve and cataloging rules change to accommodate the evolution. Ideally, catalogers should view and hear the materials they handle in order to catalog them accurately. There is no substitute for obtaining bibliographic data firsthand.

When cataloging is obtained from an outside source, such as a school district or cooperative processing center or commercial organization, librarians and media specialists should be clear about insisting, politely, that their policies be followed regarding the fullness of nonbook catalog records, rules used for description, name and subject authorities used, classification used, and so on. They should resist the suggestion that separate, nonstandard treatments for some or all nonbook formats would be easier or more efficient for young patrons. On the contrary, applying the same knowledge about one format to all of them is much easier and more efficient than learning multiple systems for different material formats.

Conclusion

Automating library catalogs has made it easier than ever to maintain a single standard stream of bibliographic products able to serve a variety of needs, among them integrated retrieval for young people who want to see "everything the library has" as well as retrieval segregated by physical format for those who seek materials in only one format, and searching by keywords using all kinds of terminology as well as by controlled subject headings using only authorized terms. What seems obvious is the goal of creating high-quality, accurate cataloging for children's nonbook materials that contains all the information needed to satisfy children's search requests. Good cataloging for children facilitates all children's ability to find what they seek among all the wonderful materials that await them in a library's collections.

Notes

1. *Anglo-American Cataloguing Rules*, 2nd ed., 2002 revision (Chicago: American Library Association, 2002).
2. AACR2, rule 1.1C1, provides two lists: one for catalogers following North American tradition and one for those following British tradition.
3. Assistance in preparing selected nonbook formats for integrated shelving or shelving in book stacks may be found in Karen C. Dreissen and Sheila A. Smyth's *A Library Manager's Guide to Physical Processing of Nonprint Materials* (Westport, CT: Greenwood Press, 1995). An earlier work with useful information is Jean Weihs's *The Integrated Library: Encouraging Access to Multimedia Materials*, 2nd ed. (Phoenix, AZ: Oryx Press, 1991).

Recommended Reading

Andrew, Paige G. *Cataloging Sheet Maps: The Basics*. New York: Haworth Information Press, 2003.

Cole, Jim, and Wayne Jones, eds. *E-serials Cataloging: Access to Continuing and Integrating Resources via the Catalog and the Web*. New York: Haworth Information Press, 2002.

Fritz, Deborah A. *Cataloging with AACR2 and MARC 21: For Books, Electronic Resources, Sound Recordings, Videorecordings, and Serials*. Chicago: American Library Association, 2004.

Hsieh-Yee, Ingrid. *Organizing Audiovisual and Electronic Resources for Access: A Cataloging Guide*. Englewood, CO: Libraries Unlimited, 2000.

McKnight, Mark. *Music Classification Systems*. Lanham, MD: Scarecrow, 2002.

Roe, Sandra K., ed. *The Audiovisual Cataloging Current*. New York: Haworth Press, 2001.

Schultz, Lois, and Sarah Shaw, eds. *Cataloging Sheet Music: Guidelines for Use with AACR2 and the MARC Format*. Lanham, MD: Scarecrow; Music Library Association, 2003.

Urbanski, Verna, et al. *Cataloging Unpublished Nonprint Materials: A Manual of Suggestions, Comments, and Examples*. Lake Crystal, MN: Soldier Creek Press, 1992.

Weber, Mary Beth. *Cataloging Nonprint and Internet Resources: A How-to-Do-It Manual for Librarians*. New York: Neal-Schuman, 2002.

Weitz, Jay. *Music Coding and Tagging: MARC 21 Content Designation for Scores and Sound Recordings*. Belle Plain, MN: Soldier Creek Press, 2001.

Helpful Websites

Authority Tools for Audiovisual and Music Catalogers: An Annotated List of Useful Resources. Robert Bratton, ed. http://www.olacinc.org/capc/authtools.html.

Online Audiovisual Catalogers. http://www.olacinc.org/capc/dvd/dvdprimer0.html.

"Original Cataloging Guide for Video Recordings" [at the University of Florida, George A. Smathers Libraries]. http://web.uflib.ufl.edu/rs/catpro/videoguide.html.

10

How the CIP Program Helps Children

Joanna F. Fountain

CIP, or Cataloging in Publication, is a cooperative program begun in 1971 by the Library of Congress in partnership with some twenty participating members of the U.S. publishing industry. Today, more than four thousand publishers participate in the CIP program. Publishers send galleys or front matter for their forthcoming books to the Library of Congress so cataloging data, prepared in advance of publication, can be printed in the book.

The CIP program attempts to cover materials that are likely to be collected by a great many U.S. libraries for which cataloging information is needed. The result is the inclusion of most monographs published in the United States. Certain materials, however, are not eligible for the CIP program, including consumable material, that is, material meant to be written in; material of a transitory nature, such as cut-out books, calendars, and phone books; textbooks below the secondary school level; music scores; mass-market paperbacks; religious instructional materials; self-published or subsidized books; and audiovisual materials. In fiscal year 2003, CIP data were provided for approximately fifty-four thousand titles.

Why Do Publishers Participate?

Publishers participate in the CIP program for several reasons. Publishers want to make their books more attractive to their library customers. Generally, when a book arrives in a library, it cannot circulate or be put on the shelf for browsing until a record is made. Books containing CIP data arrive with the intellectual work of cataloging already done, so that processing is simplified, and the books are available to the public sooner. Books published without CIP data require that someone on the library's staff produce the cataloging, find another library's cataloging record to copy, or put the book aside in the hope that either LC or another library will catalog it.

Publishers also believe that the CIP program helps them sell more books. In addition to the CIP data appearing in the book, a machine-readable version of the record is created. This is known as a MARC (Machine-Readable Cataloging) record. These MARC CIP records are distributed via the Cataloging Distribution Service (CDS) of the Library of Congress to subscribers of the MARC files. Thus, the word gets out to the library, library wholesaler, and bookstore markets that these books will soon be available. In short, CIP is another marketing tool for publishers.

Cataloging Benefits

A very high percentage of juvenile trade books are included in the CIP program. In FY03, 8,809 juvenile titles received CIP data. Library of Congress cataloging records are available for most juvenile books. Consequently, children's librarians who type their own cards have copy from which to prepare their cards as soon as the book arrives.

Libraries that purchase cataloging records from a commercial company can usually assume the cataloging they receive is based on LC cataloging. Libraries that are part of a library network and produce their catalog records from a network database will locate CIP records when they search. In short, no matter what method a library uses to produce its catalog copy, the CIP program should save it time and money, and improve the quality of its cataloging.

Because the CIP record is created from prepublication information supplied by the publisher, it must sometimes be changed after the published book is examined by a cataloger. The CIP data printed in the book are composed of selected fields from the full MARC CIP record because of space limitations on the verso of the title page for most books. At the same time that the CIP data is supplied to the publisher for printing in the book, the full cataloging record appears on the MARC files. Publishers frequently report bibliographic changes before publication, so that both the CIP data that will appear in the book and the MARC record will be accurate. Unreported changes, however, must be addressed after the book is published. With book in hand, LC staff review the MARC record and make changes as needed. However, although these unreported changes also result in some differences between the CIP data in the book, or the information on the MARC record and the information that appears on the title page and other parts of the book, they provide for more accurate information in the MARC CIP record, which is freely download-able from the Library of Congress's website: http://catalog.loc.gov. Normally, only a few changes remain. These include (1) adding the physical description (pagina-tion, presence of illustrations, and the book's dimensions); (2) deleting the 263 field (expected publication date); and (3) updating the status of the catalog record from "prepublication" to "corrected or revised." At this time, the title and statement(s) of responsibility are rechecked against the title page to ensure accuracy.

When a cataloger makes a MARC record or catalog-card set from the CIP data printed in the book, the bracketed subject headings and Dewey options—such as B, E, or Fic—will normally be used in place of the unbracketed headings and clas-sification. Name entries for individuals and groups, however, are usually the same for children's catalogs and require no change unless the book is more than a few years old, in which case some parts of the CIP may be obsolete. Name entries in CIP, as well as in other bibliographical records, may be verified for currency in the LC/NACO Name Authority File, available at http://authorities.loc.gov. Direct web access to this file—with all the names added to it by CIP catalogers—allows librar-ians to provide vastly improved access to library materials through standardized access points, in addition to simple keyword access.

Service Benefits

In addition to the time and resources saved in cataloging, the program provides service benefits. CIP data, for example, are used in book selection. As noted earlier, at the same time the record is sent to the publisher, it is also distributed to subscribers of the MARC files—book vendors, publishers, and large library networks that in turn make the CIP records available in the products and services they provide.

The Library of Congress CDS MARC Alert Service is one such service. CDS gives subscribers the opportunity to choose books that interest them from among 2,155 subject categories, including picture books for children and children's litera-ture. Each week, subscribers receive CIP records for titles that match that subject interest. Some book vendors offer similar services, although it may not be immedi-ately evident to the customer that the advance notice records of forthcoming titles are in fact CIP records.

Book vendors also use CIP records when selling books to libraries on approval. The CIP records on MARC files tell vendors what is being published and enable them to select and ship to libraries any titles that meet prearranged selection crite-ria. Appearance of CIP records on the MARC files ensures their inclusion in certain selection and review publications and consequently brings their existence to the attention of children's librarians.

CIP records are also used in public services. The summaries that appear in CIP records for children's literature are especially valuable for public service and are frequently consulted for an immediate brief description of the book's content. The summaries are also used in compiling bibliographies, preparing book talks, and—in combination with the subject headings—locating other books on a similar topic.

Conclusion

The CIP program is a useful tool for children's librarians. Perhaps this description of its possible uses will inspire librarians to be more imaginative in looking for ways in which CIP can make their jobs easier and result in more effective service.

Read More about CIP

Official LC CIP Website

> http://cip.loc.gov

Process

> http://www.ala.org/ala/aasl/aaslpubsandjournals/kqweb/kqarchives/added/32n3CIP.pdf

Information for Publishers

> http://cip.loc.gov/cipman/
> http://www.dgiinc.com/pcip.htm

Information about Canadian CIP

> http://www.collectionscanada.ca/cip/s15-1005-e.html

Some Local Guidelines for Updating CIP Data

> http://www.lib.ksu.edu/depts/techserv/manual/cataloging/monographs/cip.html
> http://web.uflib.ufl.edu/rs/catpro/catpropr870115.html
> http://library.boisestate.edu/Serials/Procedures/Standing~Orders/cipupdating.htm

11

Cataloging for Kids in the Academic Library

Gabriele I. Kupitz and Vickie Frierson-Adams

Although children do utilize academic libraries and their juvenile collections, it is the university student and his or her mentor, the academic, who are most likely to use the juvenile collections in academic settings for research purposes. The study of children's literature as a serious, scholarly discipline has long cast its net over researchers. In the 1970s, teachers and academics began to emphasize the value and the interpretation of children's literature, with particular focus on literary analysis.[1] Since that time, the study of children's literature has become a legitimate pursuit, and the corresponding scholarship has both fascinated and involved many academic institutions and their libraries.

This chapter examines current practices in the cataloging of children's materials in academic libraries and provides a report on their use gathered in a recent study.

General Observations

Because scholars use the materials in relation to teaching and research, academic libraries may opt to use Library of Congress subject headings (LCSH) and Library of Congress Classification (LCC) numbers in cataloging juvenile materials to mirror the cataloging and classification practices in place for other large scholarly collections. In addition, other bibliographic enhancements unique to research institutions are possibilities.

Computerized Catalog Records

Computer technology and serendipity are the tools of student and scholar. In the age of the online catalog, the bibliographic record offers invaluable information. The axiom "more is more" applies to the online record and the nuggets of information to be gleaned by scholars versus abbreviated computer records needed by children. Following are examples of differences that might affect typical scholarly projects.

Scrutinizing first edition titles alongside later editions of the same title holds more appeal for the scholar than for the recreational reader. Uniform titles help to identify and organize works. Exact pagination is as crucial to research as are the edition statements.

A 500 note added to the bibliographic records of picture books can highlight the art medium, type of paper, and text type used. This information is of interest to art and illustration students and their professors who peruse picture books for examples of the melding between text and art medium. In some institutions, catalogers record the art medium in genre notes.

Additional 500 notes could be used to record information found only on the dust jacket, translation information often found on the verso of the title page, copyright information, and provenance. Bibliographical references and index information are invaluable additions for students and scholars, as are summary notes, contents notes, audience notes, and the myriad of other note possibilities.

In any library, authority work is important, but in large university catalogs it is critical. Names, series, subject headings, and other access points must be as consistent as possible because of the sheer volume of records in the catalog and because of their universal potential to facilitate research. For professional academic catalogers, cataloging materials written for children requires the same attention and thoroughness as does cataloging materials for adults because these juvenile materials are for the on-site as well as the remote researcher.

Current Practices: A Report

A study was conducted in March 2000 to determine how juvenile collections in academic libraries are currently cataloged, housed, and used. Questionnaires containing fourteen items were sent to one hundred randomly selected academic catalog and technical service librarians. The response rate was 65 percent. Of the responses, four did not have a juvenile collection and one was disqualified and was not included in the survey. Thus, the following data analysis was based on the responses of sixty libraries. Because some of the respondents provided more than one answer for selected questions, some results of the study were skewed and total percentages exceed 100 percent.

Classification and Indexing of the Collection

Twenty-five libraries reported their juvenile fiction is classified using the Library of Congress Classification (LCC), excluding Juvenile Belles Lettres (LCC-PZ). Thirteen libraries said they use LCC, including the classification for Juvenile Belles Lettres. (Seventeen of those using LCC gave more than one response.) Only two of the sixty libraries reported their juvenile collection is classified using both LCC and Dewey Decimal Classification (DDC). Nineteen use DDC or a modified version.

Thirty-three of the academic libraries catalog juvenile nonfiction literature using LCC, excluding classification for Juvenile Belles Lettres. Six gave more than one response. Of these six, three classify their collection using a combination of LCC and LCC-PZ, and three use some combination of LCC and DDC. Twenty-five academic libraries use only DDC to classify juvenile nonfiction, and three use a combination of DDC and other classification schemes.

Twelve schools did not classify their juvenile collections, but used a Cuttering system to arrange the collection on the shelf. Seventy percent of the institutions surveyed said they use the same classification system for the juvenile collection as that used for the general collection.

When asked if collection labels were used in addition to the classification numbers to identify specific shelf locations, 37 percent reported using JUV (Juvenile). Others reported were J (Juvenile), CURR (Curriculum), CMC (Curriculum Materials Center), JF (Juvenile Fiction), E (Easy), FIC (fiction), CHILD COLL (Children's Collection), and YOUTH COLL (Youth Collection).

Thirty-eight percent of fifty-nine responses to a question about subject headings said they used Library of Congress subject headings (LCSH), coding them in fields 650 and 651 and using blank/0 in the indicators to indicate regular headings, not LC's Annotated Card headings. Only eleven schools used LCSH, coding the indicators both blank/0 and blank/1, with blank/1 indicating Annotated Card headings for children. Three institutions reported using Sears subject headings alone. One reported using a combination of Sears and LCSH subject headings for its juvenile collection. Three schools index their juvenile collection using a mixture of local subject headings (tagging the fields 690 and 691), regular LCSH headings, and LC Annotated Card headings for juvenile literature.

Field 710 is used to provide added entries for corporate names, but it also is used to group certain collections. Only five of the fifty-eight respondents who replied to this question used the 710 field to trace the collections.

Housing the Collection

Of sixty libraries that responded, thirty-nine revealed their collections are housed as a separate collection in the main library. Four of these thirty-nine libraries house juvenile materials in the School of Education building, and three house juvenile collections in a curriculum laboratory. Only eleven libraries interfile their collections with adult materials in the main collections.

Using the Collection

When asked which groups within the university the juvenile collection supports, 92 percent reported the Education Department. Fourteen of these respondents said the juvenile collection also provides support for the library science program. Twenty-one reported that their collections also are used by faculty and staff and their children, the community, the English literature department, and the children's literature program.

People outside the college or university also use the juvenile collections. Sixty percent said the collection is loaned to educators in the area, and 35 percent loan to their state's residents. Other outside users are home educators in the area, alumni, adults in the community, consortium borrowers, and spouses and children of faculty.

Observations on the Findings

A strong relationship exists between libraries that use LCC for juvenile fiction and nonfiction. If LCC is used for juvenile fiction, it is also used for juvenile nonfiction.

Normally, the same classification system that is used for the general collection is used for the juvenile collection (70 percent). This statistic suggests that academic libraries use LCC for all collections, with only 30 percent using a classification scheme that differs from the main collection.

Eighty percent of those surveyed use some sort of collection label for shelf location, suggesting a strong propensity to identify juvenile materials as such, with JUV being the most commonly used term. There is also a strong tendency to keep the juvenile collection materials separate from the general collection. Children's collections are housed either as a separate collection in the main library, in a curriculum lab, or in the School of Education. Eleven libraries reported that their juvenile collection is interfiled in the main collection.

The report indicates that both juvenile fiction and nonfiction are housed together in the same collection, reinforcing the cohesiveness of the collection.

The survey revealed some uniformity in assigning subject headings to juvenile collections. Eighty-five percent of respondents classify their juvenile collection using a combination of LCSH and LC Annotated Card headings for children's literature.

The responses indicate that students in the School of Education are the primary users of juvenile collections in academic libraries. Twenty-three percent of libraries reported that library science students also use them. Although most juvenile collections in academic libraries are used to support the academic curriculum and scholarship, the collection is also admired and used by parents, children, and readers outside the academic institution.

Note

1. Jill P. May, *Children's Literature and Critical Theory*, Reading and Writing for Understanding series (New York: Oxford University Press, 1995), 23.

Recommended Reading

Mann, Thomas. "Why LC Subject Headings Are More Important Than Ever," *American Libraries* 33, no. 10 (October 2003): 52–54.

Maxwell, Robert L. *Maxwell's Guide to Authority Work*. Chicago: American Library Association, 2002.

Maxwell, Robert L. *Maxwell's Handbook for AACR2: Explaining and Illustrating the Anglo-American Cataloguing Rules through the 2003 Update*. Chicago: American Library Association, 2004.

12

Automating the
Children's Catalog

Pamela J. Newberg and Judith Yurczyk

With the unrelenting advance of technology and the never-ending amount and quickening pace of the information explosion, the role of the librarian or library media specialist is continually changing. Librarians can no longer spend vast amounts of time maintaining the card catalog and keeping records manually. Libraries that have not yet introduced automation systems need to do so to provide librarians more time to assist students and teachers.

The creation of a high-quality, machine-readable database is the cornerstone of the automation process. This database is produced in a retrospective conversion process in which the entire existing catalog is converted into Machine-Readable Cataloging (MARC) records. MARC 21 is the current standard for these cataloging records. Adherence to the standard is critical if libraries are to maintain the portability of their files, allowing them to be transferred from one automated system to another without repeating the retrospective conversion phase. Standards are also essential for libraries wishing to participate in resource sharing projects with other libraries, such as the union catalogs of school districts and large consortia, and such statewide projects as the Texas Library Connection, Florida's SUNLINK, and ACCESS PENNSYLVANIA.

MARC is a communications format that provides a way to store catalog records and move them from one computer to another, but it is not a guarantee of the cataloging content. The structure of the MARC record must meet the MARC 21 standards, but the bibliographic data contained within the record should follow the Anglo-American Cataloguing Rules (AACR2). The content and quality of records may vary depending on the source of the cataloging. The Library of Congress (LC) creates high-quality MARC records. These same LC records may be available from a bibliographic utility such as OCLC or RLIN, or may be purchased from a vendor as either an online service via the Internet or a CD-ROM database. (See chapter 3 in this book for more information on the MARC format.)

Some libraries begin the automation process by introducing a circulation system for checking books in and out, keeping track of inventory, handling overdue materials, and providing reports for these functions. Circulation systems may only require brief records containing minimal information (title, author, publisher, LCCN or ISBN, call number, and bar code). Although this minimal information may be enough to track circulating items, the main reason for automating a library is to increase access to materials.

The searcher using an online catalog can obtain greater access through the use of full MARC records that offer such additional information as summaries, reading- and interest-level data, names of review sources, full physical descriptions, notes, subject headings, and other added entries.

Circulation systems and online catalogs both need to have MARC 21 records. When considering conversion options to obtain these MARC records, keep the unique information needs of young library users in mind. Sears and LC's Annotated Card program subject headings as well as Dewey call numbers are appropriate for children's catalogs, as are summaries, reading and interest levels, and so on. Many vendors enhance LC's MARC records with this additional information.

Obtaining the MARC Database

You can obtain MARC records for your online catalog and circulation system in several ways, including full-service vendor conversion, joint in-house/vendor conversion, full in-house conversion, and manual entry. These formats are discussed in the sections that follow.

Full-Service Vendor Conversion. Send a catalog card (preferably a shelflist card or a copy of the title page) for each item in your library to a vendor who will match the title against its database and provide MARC records on disks or tapes or via FTP (file transfer protocol). The cost of this method varies depending on the type of MARC records you receive. For example, brief records cost less than full MARC records. Audiovisual materials are more difficult and expensive to convert than are printed materials (additional fields and multiple fixed-length fields are often required). Some vendors will create a MARC record for nonhits (no match in the vendor's database) using information contained on a library's shelflist card. Other vendors return nonhits for libraries to create their own records.

Joint In-House/Vendor Conversion. Enter brief data (LCCN or ISBN or both, title, and your local information) for each item in your collection onto paper or a disk. The vendor will run these brief data against its database looking for matches. The vendor then provides full MARC records for the hits (MARC records that match the LCCN or ISBN) on disks or tapes or via FTP to be loaded into your system, and the library staff will need to create MARC records for the nonhits.

Full In-House Conversion. Subscribe to an online service and access millions of MARC records over the Internet or purchase a CD-ROM product on which you can search to find records matching the titles in your collection. You can download these matching records onto disks or tapes or directly into your online catalog. Follett's Alliance Plus and AV ACCESS, Athena's CD Cataloger, the Library Corporation's Its.MARC, and Brodart's Precision One are examples of online services that provide millions of MARC records and let local libraries perform their own retrospective conversion. Library staff also create records for the nonhits.

You can obtain MARC 21 records via the Internet using either the World Wide Web or the Z39.50 protocol. With Z39.50 you can search various databases from other libraries that do not necessarily use the same software you do and download matching MARC records into your database. The entire Library of Congress database is accessible and free for downloading to any library either through direct web access or the Z39.50 protocol. Some library software systems include this capability, but if the automation system or software you choose does not, other products, such as Book Where and eZ-Cat, allow you to download MARC records from the Library of Congress, university catalogs, and large public libraries with Z39.50 servers. Downloaded records can be used with any automation system that accepts MARC 21 records, such as Athena, Alexandria, Bibliofile, Dynix, Follett, Spectrum, Verso, and many others.

Manual Entry. Purchase library automation software and you, your staff, or volunteers can create MARC records by entering data from your catalog card into a template in your online catalog system. Many software vendors now provide entry templates for users without MARC knowledge as well as for users who are already familiar with MARC standards. Mitinet's MARC Magician, which complements all MARC-based automation systems, provides easy original cataloging templates, with English prompts, on-screen tips, and examples to help you enter MARC records. It is important to have a copy of the current edition of the *Anglo-American Cataloguing Rules* handy in either case, as MARC protocols are concerned with the structure rather than the content of cataloging records.

No one method is superior to another. The method you choose will depend on the size of your collection, your budget, amount of time available, and the knowledge level of your library's staff.

Additional Tasks

In addition to creating MARC records, the automation process includes bar coding of each item for circulation and inventory purposes. To save time, pre–bar code your collection either during inventory or as you weed the collection and prepare it for automation. Some data cleanup is always necessary after a retrospective conversion. This may include creating records for unmatched items, changing local information regarding the number of copies and volumes for certain items, changing call numbers, or standardizing subject and name headings. Cleanup may be done manually but can be very time consuming. A product such as MARC Magician, which uses built-in MARC 21 rules and variables, helps clean up MARC records as it automatically corrects many structural errors, such as punctuation and nonfiling indicators for initial articles (*A, An, The, Los, Las,* etc.), when records are imported into the program.

Another and perhaps the most important part of the automation process is selecting the automation system. Each library has its own needs and budget constraints, but with vastly increasing record sharing, the importance of the system you choose reaches beyond local concerns. Many vendors now offer some type of web-based access to a library's catalog, allowing for searching entire library collections from anywhere and at any time as well as searching other library catalogs within a district or consortium. Before making a final decision, you might want to talk with other librarians in your area to learn the strengths and weaknesses of the systems they use.

Ongoing Concerns

Now you have your library automated. What's next?

The database of MARC records must be maintained. Several sources provide MARC records for new titles. Many vendors now sell MARC records with materials purchased from them and will provide complete processing, including spine labels, catalog cards for a manual shelflist (if one is still maintained), MARC records, bar codes, and book jackets. When purchasing MARC records from a vendor, make sure the specifications given to the vendor match your system's technical requirements (see chapter 13 for additional information). Before loading the records into the local system, preview them to ensure that information you requested in your data profile is included and that authority work was done on the name and subject headings. A good way to do this is to run them through MARC Magician, which will automatically correct some MARC errors and will report predefined errors and omissions through the Active Error Checking feature. After records are loaded into the local system, items are placed on the shelves, and shelflist cards are filed.

Some vendors will provide MARC records for titles not purchased from them. This is helpful for titles purchased from vendors who do not offer MARC records or who do not have staff who can produce good MARC records, and for titles that may be donated to the library or purchased locally.

Another source of new MARC records is a vendor specializing in MARC records. Some vendors produce MARC records on CD-ROM (such as Alliance Plus and Its.MARC). Another source is a database utility (such as OCLC or RLIN, or Auto-Graphics) in which MARC records are contributed by member libraries. Yet another growing source is computer programs that download selected MARC records from the Internet and allow editing of the records before importing them into the local automation system. All these sources operate on a subscription basis; some may be more cost effective for larger libraries or systems. Another option, of course, is to catalog items yourself using the standard tools: AACR2, MARC 21, Dewey, and LC Annotated Card program or Sears subject heading lists.

Whichever option you choose, you need to know your automation system's requirements for importing or creating MARC records. The most important requirement is to know which field contains the holdings information and how that must be coded. If you use vendor-supplied MARC records, make sure each vendor has the same information. All vendors should know the placement of local notes and other notes, such as reading and interest levels and awards notes, and whether these notes are indexed. How the automation system indexes such information as series headings (some systems do not index 800 or 830 fields) also affects how the MARC records are edited before import. MARC formats and coding change from time to time. Know how the vendors of your MARC records and the automation system incorporate these changes.

Authority control within the automation system is also important (see chapter 5 for a more detailed explanation of authority control). If the automation system has authority control, learn the reporting features and develop a system of checking and correcting errors so that the patrons have an easier time using the catalog. If your system does not have authority control, make sure that MARC records purchased from a vendor are subject to strict authority control before they are sent to you. Also check with the vendor to determine how quickly changes in subject headings, name headings, and call numbers are incorporated into its MARC records.

When changes occur, especially to subject headings, you will need to determine how these changes will be incorporated into your catalog. If an automated system uses *see* and *see also* references as part of the authority control, a *see also* reference can be created to guide patrons to further or related headings. If the automation system has global change capabilities, outdated headings can be easily corrected; otherwise, you may need to change each heading individually.

Conclusion

It is impossible to ever really finish your MARC database. Automating your collection and maintaining a high-quality database of MARC records can sometimes seem like a chore, but it is critical to ensuring that your teachers and students enjoy the greatest access to library resources. The quality of your data directly determines the success of their searches. In this age of information overload, an even stronger need exists to provide a single place for teachers and students to search for all the information they seek. Your library catalog can be a gateway to all the information available—if you keep your database in order.

Recommended Reading

Sager, Donald J. *Small Libraries: Organization and Operation*. 3rd ed. Fort Atkinson, WI: Highsmith, 2000.

Understanding MARC Authority Records: Machine-Readable Cataloging. Washington, DC: Library of Congress, 2004. http://www.loc.gov/marc/uma/index.html.

Understanding MARC Bibliographic: Machine-Readable Cataloging. Washington, DC: Library of Congress, 2003. http://www.loc.gov/marc/umb.

13

Vendors of Cataloging for Children's Materials

Pamela J. Newberg and Jennifer Allen

Many libraries purchase cataloging from a vendor to save time and money. An initial expenditure of time on the part of the librarian can greatly enhance the entire experience as well as the resulting cataloging (and, often, the processing) product.

Where to get cataloging is the first consideration, and several sources are available. Three major categories are (1) book wholesalers or prebinders, (2) cataloging service or software vendors, and (3) bibliographic utilities.

Wholesalers and prebinders. Hundreds of book and audiovisual wholesalers and book prebinding companies exist, and most offer some sort of cataloging or processing or both for materials purchased from them. Some also offer cataloging for materials they sell but that may not have been purchased directly from them.

Cataloging vendors. Some vendors offer cataloging products and services either online or on CD-ROM. There are also software programs that download MARC records using the Z39.50 protocol (see chapter 12 for more details).

Bibliographic utilities. Not-for-profit bibliographic networks, such as OCLC, also called bibliographic utilities, use computer databases of member-supplied cataloging records. Libraries using these services sign a membership agreement, often arranged through a local or regional library network.

Whichever route you take, a thorough evaluation of the collection will aid considerably in the process. This is critical if the chosen vendor will be cataloging and processing materials purchased. The basic choices are Dewey or LC call numbers and LC or Sears subject headings. Then the choices get a bit more complicated.

Call Numbers

Questions regarding call numbers involve policies covering the assignment of classification numbers and the addition of book numbers. If Dewey is used

> Should the source be the abridged edition or the unabridged edition?
>
> Are the numbers carried to the first slash? Two digits past the decimal? Four digits past the decimal?
>
> Are author letters or Cutter numbers used? If so, how many characters or digits will be assigned?
>
> Where are the biographies? 921? B? Will they be shelved in a separate section or mixed with other nonfiction?
>
> Where are easy books? Are they marked E or P, or something else?
>
> Are there special collections that require a prefix (Reference, Professional collection, Foreign language, Story collections)?
>
> If automated, in which tag and subfield divisions do the call numbers belong?

Subject Headings

Questions about subject headings include the following:

> What subject authority will be used: LC adult headings, AC headings (LC children's headings), or Sears?
>
> Are the numbers of subject headings used limited in some way?

Reading Programs

Special treatments to facilitate reading programs require asking the following:

> If a reading program is used, how are the books identified?
>
> If automated, are there special requirements for this tag?

Physical Processing

Choices about physical processing include decisions about the following:

> Covers or not?
>
> Cards and pockets?
>
> Bar codes? If so, where will they be placed on the materials?

Armed with this information, vendors can be selected who meet most of these needs. Ask potential vendors

Where do they obtain their cataloging records?

Are the cataloging records reviewed? Are they reviewed by professional catalogers?

Does every MARC record have an annotation or summary note?

How do they handle updates in cataloging practice, call numbers, and subject headings?

Do they use authority files? If so, which authority files are used and how are they maintained?

Which descriptive cataloging standards do they follow? If they use AACR2, which bibliographic level will be chosen?

What procedure is used if a question arises about specifications, cataloging, or processing?

What is the procedure for special cataloging requests?

Are cataloging specifications kept on file, or must they be submitted with each order?

How are MARC records sent to the library?

If more than one vendor is selected, be sure that each one receives the same specifications for your collection.

The process does not end once a vendor has been selected, specifications have been recorded and filed, and materials are received. The cataloging record, whether on cards or in a computer file, should be reviewed for completeness, accuracy, and the library's specific collection and call number requests. The vendor should also be periodically evaluated for adherence to bibliographic standards and implementation of changes in standard cataloging practice, call numbers, or subject headings. Evaluation should be ongoing to ensure that children or adults using the catalog will always receive high-quality service.

Directory of Vendors

U.S. and Canadian Wholesalers and Prebinders Offering Cataloging Services

Baker and Taylor
2550 West Tyvola Rd., Ste. 300
Charlotte, NC 28217
1-800-775-1800
btinfo@btol.com

Blackwell's Book Services
6024 Jean Rd., Bldg. G
Lake Oswego, OR 97035
1-800-547-6426
custserv@blackwell.com

Book Wholesalers, Inc.
1847 Mercer Rd.
Lexington, KY 40511
1-800-888-4478
custservice@bwibooks.com

The BookSource, Inc.
1230 Macklind Ave.
St. Louis, MO 63110
1-800-444-0435
info@booksource.com

Bound to Stay Bound Books, Inc.
1880 West Morton Rd.
Jacksonville, IL 62650
1-800-637-6586
btsb@btsb.com

Brodart Books
500 Arch St.
Williamsport, PA 17701
1-800-474-9802
bookscs@brodart.com

Coutts Library Services, Inc.
1823 Maryland Ave.
Niagara Falls, NY 14302-1000
1-800-263-1686
ehorvath@couttsinfo.com

Demco/Turtleback Books
P.O. Box 14260
Madison, WI 53708
1-800-448-8939
turtleback@demco.com

Econo-Clad Books
3601 Minnesota Dr., Ste. 550
Minneapolis, MN 55435
1-800-328-2923
info@sagebrushcorp.com

Follett Library Resources
1340 Ridgeview Dr.
McHenry, IL 60050
1-888-511-5114
customerservice@flr.follett.com

Ingram Library Services
One Ingram Blvd.
LaVergne, TN 37086-1986
1-800-937-5300
reply@library.info.ingram.book.com

Mackin Library Media
615 Travelers Trail West
Burnsville, MN 55337
1-800-245-9540
mackinbk@mr.net

Mook and Blanchard
546 Hofgaarden St.
La Puente, CA 91744
1-800-875-9911
cust@mookandblanchard.com

National Book Service
25 Kodiak Crescent
Toronto, Ontario M3J 3M5
Canada
1-800-387-3178
nbs@nbs.com

Perma-Bound Books
617 E. Vandalia Rd.
Jacksonville, IL 62650
1-800-637-6581
books@perma-bound.com

Quality Books
1003 West Pines Rd.
Oregon, IL 61061-9680
1-800-323-4241
http://www.quality-books.com

S and B Books, Ltd.
3085 Universal Dr.
Mississauga, Ontario L4X 2E2
Canada
1-800-997-7099

Story House Corp.
Bindery Ln.
Charlotteville, NY 12036
1-800-847-2105
http://www.story-house.com

Bibliographic Utilities and Companies Offering Cataloging Production and Services

Amigos Library Services
14400 Midway Rd.
Dallas, TX 75244-3509
1-800-843-8482
amigos@amigos.org

Auto-Graphics, Inc.
3201 Temple Ave.
Pomona, CA 91768
1-800-776-6939

Book Systems, Inc.
721 Clinton Ave., Ste. 11
Huntsville, AL 35801
1-888-289-1216
http://www.booksys.com

Brodart Automation
500 Arch St.
Williamsport, PA 17705
1-800-233-8467, ext. 6581

Catalog Card Company
12221 Wood Lake Dr.
Burnsville, MN 55337
1-800-328-2923

Duncan Systems Specialists
281 Wyecroft Rd.
Oaksville, Ontario L6K 2H2
Canada
1-800-836-5049
dss@duncansystems.com

Follett Software Company
1391 Corporate Dr.
McHenry, IL 60050-7041
1-800-323-3397
http://www.fsc.follett.com

Gaylord Information Systems
P.O. Box 490
Syracuse, NY 13221-4901
1-800-272-3414
gisinfo@gaylord.com

Library Associates
FastCat Cataloging Division
8845 W. Olympic Blvd., Ste. 201
Beverly Hills, CA 90211
1-800-987-6794
fastcat@primenet.com

Library Conversions Limited Co.
5010 East Shea Blvd., Bldg. A, Ste. 214A
Scottsdale, AZ 85254
1-800-268-9278
http://www.libraryconversions.com

Library Data Services
Box 1054
Stouffville, Ontario L4A 8A1
Canada
1-905-640-3716
caromori@enoreo.on.ca

Library of Congress
101 Independence Ave., SE
Washington, DC 20541-4912
1-800-255-3666
cdsinfo@loc.gov

London West Resource Centre
708 Gideon Dr.
London, Ontario N6P 1P2
1-519-471-4921; 1-800-387-5958

The MARC of Quality
5880-A Highway A1A
Melbourne Beach, FL 32951
1-800-560-MARC (6272)
tmq@marcofquality.com

MARCIVE, Inc.
P.O. Box 47508
San Antonio, TX 78265-7508
1-800-531-7678
info@marcive.com

OCLC
6565 Frantz Rd.
Dublin, OH 43017-3395
1-800-848-5878
http://www.oclc.org

OCLC Western Service Center
4224 6th Ave. SE, Bldg. 3
Lacey, WA 98503-1040
1-800-854-5753
http://www.wln.com

Sagebrush Library Services
2101 N. Topeka Blvd.
Topeka, KS 66608
1-800-442-7332
http://www.sagebrushcorp.com/
    dataservices

SOLINET
1438 W. Peachtree St. NW, Ste. 200
Atlanta, GA 30309-2955
1-800-999-8558
solinet_information@soline

TLC The Library Corporation
Research Park
Inwood, WV 25428-9733
1-304-229-0100; 1-800-325-7759
info@TLCdelivers.com

Glossary of Acronyms

Joanna F. Fountain and Sheila S. Intner

AACR2	*Anglo-American Cataloguing Rules*, 2nd edition
AC	Annotated Card [program of the Library of Congress]
ALA	American Library Association
ALCTS	Association for Library Collections and Technical Services [a division of the American Library Association]
ASCII	American Standard Code for Information Interchange
AUSMARC	Australian MARC
BT	broader term
CANMARC	Canadian MARC
CARL	Colorado Alliance of Research Libraries
CatSIG	Cataloging Special Interest Group
CCM	Canadian Committee on MARC
CCS	Cataloging and Classification Section [of the Association for Library Collections and Technical Services]
CD-ROM	compact disc read-only memory
CDS	Cataloging Distribution Service [Library of Congress]
CILIP	Chartered Institute of Library and Information Professionals [formerly the (British) Library Association]
CIP	Cataloging in Publication
DC	Dewey Classification
DCD	Decimal Classification Division [Library of Congress]
DDC	Dewey Decimal Classification
DOS	Disk Operating System
DVD	digital videodisc
EPC	Editorial Policy Committee [of Dewey Decimal Classification]
FRBR	*Functional Requirements for Bibliographic Records*

FTP	File Transfer Protocol
GMD	general material designation
ICDL	International Children's Digital Library
ISBD	International Standard Bibliographic Description
ISBN	International Standard Book Number
ISSN	International Standard Serial Number
LAC	Library and Archives Canada [formerly National Library of Canada]
LC	Library of Congress
LC MARC	original version of MARC, instituted by the Library of Congress
LC/NACO	Library of Congress/name authority component [of the Program for Cooperative Cataloging]
LCC	Library of Congress Classification
LCCN	Library of Congress Control Number
LCC-PZ	Library of Congress Classification schedule for Juvenile Belles Lettres
LCRI	*Library of Congress Rule Interpretations*
LC/SACO	Library of Congress/subject authority component [of the Program for Cooperative Cataloging]
LCSH	*Library of Congress Subject Headings*
MARBI	Committee on Representation in Machine-Readable Form of Bibliographic Information [of the American Library Association]
MARC	Machine-Readable Cataloging
MARC 21	first international version of the MARC standards
NACO	name authority component of the Library of Congress Program for Cooperative Cataloging
NAF	Name Authority File
NT	narrower term
OCLC	Online Computer Library Center [formerly Ohio College Library Center]
OCLC MARC	a version of MARC designed by and for OCLC
OPAC	Online Public Access Catalog
PCC	Program for Cooperative Cataloging
RLG	Research Libraries Group
RLIN	Research Libraries Information Network
RT	related term
RTSD	Resources and Technical Services Division [of the American Library Association]

SAC	Subject Analysis Committee [of the Cataloging and Classification Section of the Association for Library Collections and Technical Services]
SUNLINK	Florida's K–12 public school union catalog
UF	used for
UK	United Kingdom
UNIMARC	Universal Machine-Readable Cataloging [an international version of MARC devised before MARC 21]
URL	uniform resource locator
USMARC	United States MARC
Utlas	University of Toronto Libraries Automated System
WebPac	online public access catalog
XML	Extensible Markup Language

Bibliography

Virginia M. Overberg and Brigid Burke

Primary Tools

General Manuals

Chan, Lois Mai. *Cataloging and Classification: An Introduction.* 2nd ed. New York: McGraw-Hill, 1993.

Ferguson, Bobby. *Cataloging Nonprint Materials: Blitz Cataloging Workbook.* Englewood, CO: Libraries Unlimited, 1999.

Hoffman, Herbert H. *Small Library Cataloging.* 3rd ed. Lanham, MD: Scarecrow, 2002.

IFLANET. *Digital Libraries: Cataloging and Indexing of Electronic Resources.* http://www.ifla.org/II/catalog.htm.

Intner, Sheila S., and Jean Weihs. *Standard Cataloging for School and Public Libraries.* 3rd ed. Englewood, CO: Libraries Unlimited, 2001.

Library of Congress. *Cataloger's Desktop.* http://desktop.loc.gov.

Olson, Nancy B., ed. *Cataloging of Internet Resources: A Manual and Practical Guide.* http://www.oclc.org/support/documentation/worldcat/cataloging/internetguide.

Pennell, Charlie, and Suzanne Ellison. *Cataloguer's Toolbox.* http://staff.library.mun.ca/staff/toolbox.

Taylor, Arlene G. *Wynar's Introduction to Cataloging and Classification.* 9th ed. Littleton, CO: Libraries Unlimited, 2000.

The Library Corporation. *Cataloger's Reference Shelf.* http://www.itsmarc.com/crs/CRS0000.htm.

Weber, Mary Beth. *Cataloging Nonprint and Internet Resources: A How-to-Do-It Manual for Librarians.* New York: Neal-Schuman, 2002.

Descriptive Cataloging

Anglo-American Cataloguing Rules. 2nd ed., 2002 rev. and updates. Chicago: American Library Association, 2002–.

Fritz, Deborah A. *Cataloging with AACR2 and MARC21: For Books, Electronic Resources, Sound Recordings, Videorecordings, and Serials*. Chicago: American Library Association, 2004.

Gorman, Michael. *The Concise AACR2*. Chicago: American Library Association, 2004.

Haynes, Elizabeth, and Joanna F. Fountain. *Unlocking the Mysteries of Cataloging: A Workbook of Examples*. Westport, CT: Libraries Unlimited, 2005.

Maxwell, Robert L. *Maxwell's Handbook for AACR2: Explaining and Illustrating the Anglo-American Cataloguing Rules through the 2003 Update*. Chicago: American Library Association, 2004.

Mortimer, Mary. *Learn Descriptive Cataloging*. Lanham, MD: Scarecrow, 2000.

MARC Format

Byrne, Deborah J. *MARC Manual: Understanding and Using MARC Records*. 2nd ed. Englewood, CO: Libraries Unlimited, 1998.

Ferguson, Bobby. *MARC/AACR2/Authority Control Tagging: Blitz Cataloging Workbook*. 2nd ed. Westport, CT: Libraries Unlimited, 2005.

Furrie, Betty. *Understanding MARC Bibliographic: Machine-Readable Cataloging*. 7th ed. Washington, DC: Library of Congress, Cataloging Distribution Service, 2003.

Furrie, Betty, in conjunction with the Data Base Development Department of the Follett Software Company. *Understanding MARC Bibliographic*. 7th ed. http://lcweb.loc.gov/marc/umb.

Library of Congress. Network Development and MARC Standards Office. *MARC Standards*. http://lcweb.loc.gov/marc.

MARC 21 Format for Bibliographic Data. Washington, DC: Library of Congress, 1999.

Maxwell, Robert L. *Maxwell's Guide to Authority Work*. Chicago: American Library Association, 2002.

Understanding MARC Authority Records: Machine-Readable Cataloging. Washington, DC: Library of Congress, Cataloging Distribution Service, 2004. http://www.loc.gov/marc/uma/index.html.

Classification

Chan, Lois Mai. *A Guide to the Library of Congress Classification*. 5th ed. Englewood, CO: Libraries Unlimited, 1999.

Dewey, Melvil. *Abridged Dewey Decimal Classification and Relative Index*. Edited by Joan S. Mitchell, Julianne Beall, Winton E. Matthews Jr., and Gregory R. New. 14th ed. Albany, NY: OCLC Forest Press, 2004.

————. *Dewey Decimal Classification and Relative Index*. Edited by Joan S. Mitchell, Julianne Beall, Winton E. Matthews Jr., and Gregory R. New. 22nd ed. Albany, NY: OCLC Forest Press, 2003.

Library of Congress. *ClassWeb*. http://classweb.loc.gov.

Library of Congress. Subject Cataloging Division. *LC Classification Outline*. 7th ed. Washington, DC: Library of Congress, 2003.

McKnight, Mark. *Music Classification Systems*. Lanham, MD: Scarecrow, 2002.

Mortimer, Mary. *Learn Dewey Decimal Classification*. Lanham, MD: Scarecrow, 1999.

————. *Learn Library of Congress Classification*. Lanham, MD: Scarecrow, 1999.

OCLC. *Dewey Decimal Classification—New and Changed Entries*. http://www.oclc .org/dewey/updates/new.

————. *Dewey Decimal Classification—Tips*. http://www.oclc.org/dewey/updates /tips/default.htm.

————. *WebDewey*. http://connexion.oclc.org/corc.html.

Scott, Mona L. *Dewey Decimal Classification, 22nd Edition: A Study Manual and Number Building Guide*. Westport, CT: Libraries Unlimited, 2005.

Subject Headings

Bilindex General: A List of Spanish-English Bilingual Subject Heading Equivalents to Library of Congress Subject Heading List. Mountain View, CA: Inter American Development/Floricanto Press, 2004.

Chan, Lois Mai. *Library of Congress Subject Headings: Principles and Application*, 2nd ed. Englewood, CO: Libraries Unlimited, 2005.

Ferguson, Bobby. *Subject Analysis: Blitz Cataloging Workbook*. Englewood, CO: Libraries Unlimited, 1998.

Fountain, Joanna F. *Subject Headings for School and Public Libraries: An LCSH/Sears Companion*. 3rd ed. Englewood, CO: Libraries Unlimited, 2001.

Library and Archives Canada. *Canadian Subject Headings* (CSH). http://www.collections canada.ca/csh/index-e.html.

Library of Congress. *Library of Congress Authorities*. http://authorities.loc.gov.

————. *Moving Image Genre-Form Guide*. http://lcweb.loc.gov/rr/mopic/ miggen.html.

————. Subject Cataloging Division. *Library of Congress Subject Headings*. 28th ed. Washington, DC: Library of Congress, 2005.

Mortimer, Mary. *Learn Library of Congress Subject Access*. Lanham, MD: Scarecrow, 2000.

Sears List of Subject Headings. 18th ed. Edited by Joseph Miller. New York: H. W. Wilson, 2004.

Sears List of Subject Headings: Canadian Companion. 6th ed. Edited by Lynne Lighthall. New York: H. W. Wilson, 2001.

Sears Lista de Encabezamientos de Materia. Translated by Carmen Rovira. New York: H. W. Wilson, 1984.

Subject Headings for Children: A List of Subject Headings Used by Library of Congress with Dewey Numbers Added. Edited by Lois Winkel. 2 vols. Albany, NY: Forest Press, 1998.

Filing

ALA Filing Rules. Chicago: American Library Association, 1980.

Carothers, Diane Foxhill. *Self-Instruction Manual for Filing Catalog Cards.* Washington, DC: Library of Congress, 1981.

Library of Congress Filing Rules. Prepared by John C. Rather and Susan C. Biebel. Washington, DC: Library of Congress, 1980.

Cataloging for Children

Boyce, Judith I., and Bert R. Boyce. "A Reexamination of Shelf Organization for Children's Books." *Public Libraries* (September/October 2002): 280–83.

Children's Catalog. 18th ed. New York: H. W. Wilson, 2001–.

Frierson-Adams, Vickie. "Cataloging Juvenile Monographs in an Academic Library." *Technical Services Quarterly* 20, no. 1 (2002): 39–47.

Jacobson, Frances F. "From Dewey to Mosaic: Considerations in Interface Design for Children." *Internet Research* 5, no. 2 (1995): 67–73.

McCroskey, Marilyn, and Michelle R. Turvey. "Frequently Asked Questions on CIP." *Knowledge Quest* 32, no. 4 (March/April 2004): 39–40.

———. "Processing New CIP Materials at the Library of Congress." *Knowledge Quest* 32, no. 3 (January/February 2004): 38–39.

Middle and Junior High School Library Catalog. 8th ed. Edited by Anne Price and Juliette Yaakov. New York: H. W. Wilson, 2000–.

Vizine-Goetz, Diane. "Popular LCSH with Dewey Numbers: Subject Headings for Everyone." *Journal of Library Administration* 34, no. 3/4 (2001): 293–99.

Woodbury, Sara. "Subject Access to Children's Picture Books." *Technicalities* 23, no. 2 (March/April 2003): 8–12.

Further Reading and Study

Akers, Susan Grey. *Akers' Simple Library Cataloging.* 7th ed. Revised and rewritten by Arthur Curley and Jana Varlejs. Metuchen, NJ: Scarecrow, 2003.

"Annotated Card Program: AC Subject Headings." In *Library of Congress Subject Headings*, 27th ed., xix–xxxvi. Washington, DC: Library of Congress, Cataloging Policy and Support Division, 2004.

Ballard, Terry. *Typographical Errors in Library Databases*. Revised January 2005. http://faculty.quinnipiac.edu/libraries/tballard/typoscomplete.html.

Borgman, Christine L., Sandra G. Hirsch, and Virginia A. Walter. "Children's Searching Behavior on Browsing and Keyword Online Catalogs: The Science Library Catalog Project." *Journal of the American Society for Information Science* 46, no. 9 (October 1995): 663–84.

Drabenstott, Karen M., and Marjorie S. Weller. "Handling Spelling Errors in Online Catalog Searches." *Library Resources and Technical Services* 40, no. 2 (April 1996): 113–32.

Foskett, A. C. *The Subject Approach to Information*. 5th ed. London: The Library Association, 1996.

Hagler, Ronald. *The Bibliographic Record and Information Technology*. 3rd ed. Chicago: American Library Association, 1997.

Librarians' Index to the Internet. http://lii.org.

The Librarian's Yellow Pages. Larchmont, NY: Garance, 2003.

The Librarian's Yellow Pages. http://www.librariansyellowpages.com.

Library Journal's Buyer's Guide and Web Site Directory. http://sourcebook .cahners1.com/libjrn.

Library of Congress. *Online Catalog*. http://catalog.loc.gov/webvoy.htm.

Morrill, Martha. "Roles 2000: How to Contain an Ever Expanding Job." *School Library Journal* 41, no. 1 (January 1995): 32–34.

Northern Lights Internet Solutions. *Publishers' Catalogues*. http://www.lights.com/ publisher.

OLAC (Online Audiovisual Catalogers). http://www.olacinc.org.

Outsourcing Cataloging, Authority Work, and Physical Processing: A Checklist of Considerations. Chicago: American Library Association, 1995.

Stine, Diane. "Retrospective Conversion Projects." *Media and Methods* (September/October 1996): 33.

Contributors

Jennifer Allen is Supervisor of Cataloging and Collection Development at Perma-Bound Books in Jacksonville, Illinois. She finds her work as a former English teacher and school librarian indispensable when working with customers at Perma-Bound. She is presently working on her master's degree in library and information science through the University of Missouri, Columbia. She lives in Ashland, Illinois, with her husband, Steve, and two children, Jeffrey and Carrie.

Brigid Burke is the Application Librarian/Assistant Director for the Morris County (New Jersey) Office of Library Information Systems, where she formerly served as Head of Cataloging. Currently, she is the Project Manager and Data Conversion Specialist for the Morris County (New Jersey) Automated Information Network's library system migration. Brigid has been cataloging for the last eleven years at a variety of institutions (public, school, academic, and vendor) and is an adjunct professor of cataloging at Rutgers University in New Brunswick, New Jersey. She teaches cataloging workshops for regional library cooperatives and is currently a member of the PALINET Board of Trustees. Previously, she served as President of the New Jersey Library Association Technical Services section. Outside work, Brigid volunteers as a therapist for cancer patients at Morristown Memorial Hospital in Morristown, New Jersey.

Joanna F. Fountain has worked in libraries and publishing since the early 1960s. After graduating with majors in Spanish and library science, she first worked with children on the bookmobiles in San Antonio, Texas. She has been an elementary school librarian, special librarian, editor, and academic library department head, using her Spanish bilingual skills in each position. She began consulting in 1990, and since then has organized the resource collections of two state agency libraries and a rehabilitation center. In addition to cataloging audiovisual materials on a contract basis, she serves Texas schools as liaison for the K–12 union catalog, conducts workshops, writes, and teaches graduate-level courses in technical services and cataloging in person and online. Joanna hopes this publication will help to raise awareness of the special responsibilities of those who catalog for developing readers and the researchers of the future.

Vickie Frierson-Adams is Catalog/Database Maintenance Librarian and a tenured assistant professor at the John Davis Williams Library at the University of Mississippi, Oxford Campus. She received a bachelor of business administration degree from the University of Mississippi and a master of library and information science degree from the University of Southern Mississippi, Hattiesburg, with a specialization in juvenile literature. Vickie is the former chairperson of the Juvenile Collection Committee at the John Davis Williams Library. She has published articles in *Technical Services Quarterly* and the *Southeastern Librarian*, both peer-reviewed journals, as well as articles and book reviews in *Mississippi Libraries.* Before assuming her current position, Vickie served as Circulation Librarian at the University of Mississippi's Eastland Law Library.

Deborah A. Fritz is the co-owner of The MARC of Quality, a Florida-based company that provides training, software, and database services to help librarians create better MARC records. Formerly a cataloging trainer at a multitype library consortium, and before that head of retrospective conversion at a large bibliographic utility and a cataloger at various libraries, she currently teaches an extensive array of cataloging workshops around the United States and abroad. Deborah is the author of *Cataloging with AACR2 and MARC 21*, coauthor of *MARC 21 for Everyone*, and codeveloper of several MARC processing programs ("MARC Report," "MARC Global"). She earned her master's degree in library science at the University of Toronto.

Jane E. Gilchrist is the Head of the Children's Literature cataloging team at the Library of Congress. She has served on the Cataloging of Children's Materials Committee of the Cataloging and Classification Section of the Association for Library Collections and Technical Services in various capacities and is the Library of Congress liaison to the Committee. She is also on the advisory board of the International Children's Digital Library. She has written about the Annotated Card program in previous editions of *Cataloging Correctly for Kids.*

Sheila S. Intner is professor emerita in the Graduate School of Library and Information Science, Simmons College, and teaches collection development, technical services, user instruction, and professional writing. She was founding director of the GSLIS master's degree program in library and information science at Mount Holyoke College, South Hadley, Massachusetts, a position from which she retired in 2002. Sheila received the Association for Library Collections and Technical Services Cataloging and Classification Section (ALCTS/CCS) Margaret Mann Citation Award in 1997 and the New England Technical Services Librarians Annual Award in 2003, and was named 2003 Distinguished Alumna by Queens College's Department of Library and Information Science. She has been a Fulbright Scholar to Israel, Germany, and the Republic of Georgia, and was sent to Indonesia in 2004 by the U.S. Department of State and the Institute for Training and Development–Amherst. Sheila is the author or principal editor of nineteen books and dozens of articles in both the popular and scholarly press. She has served as editor of *Library Resources and Technical Services* (1986–1990) and *Technicalities* (1992–2001) and is editor of the ALA Editions monograph series Frontiers of Access to Library Materials. She currently writes the "Dollars and Sense" column for *Technicalities.*

Lynne A. Jacobsen is Head of Technical Services at Warren-Newport Public Library, Gurnee, Illinois, where she has worked since 1994. She also catalogs at the College of Lake County (Illinois) and teaches cataloging and classification for the Library Technical Assistant program. Previously, she was a cataloger at Cook Memorial Public Library in Libertyville, Illinois. Lynne received her undergraduate degree in physical education from the University of Illinois, Urbana-Champaign, and her MLIS from Northern Illinois University. She previously served as intern to the Cataloging of Children's Materials Committee in 1995–96 and contributed a chapter to the third edition of *Cataloging Correctly for Kids.* She has also published an article titled "Warren-Newport: Testing Innovative Design Concepts" in the *ILA Reporter,* February 1998.

Gabriele "Gabi" I. Kupitz is a librarian in the Harold B. Lee Library at Brigham Young University in Provo, Utah. She catalogs juvenile literature and special collections materials.

Kay E. Lowell is Professor, University Libraries, and Archival Services Librarian at the James A. Michener Library of the University of Northern Colorado in Greeley. She has been employed at UNC since 1993 and was Catalog Librarian and Manager of the Catalog Department from 1994 to 2005. Her MLS is from the State University of New York at Buffalo. She has worked in public, health sciences, and both small and medium-sized academic libraries, cataloging all formats of materials, with special assignments in medical cataloging, children's literature and instructional resources cataloging, music cataloging, and authority control. A doctoral student in instructional design and educational technology, she has also taught master's level cataloging courses as well as individual workshops. She was a member of the Cataloging of Children's Materials Committee of ALCTS-CCS from 1999 to 2004 and was its chairperson from 2003 to 2004.

Joseph Miller is Associate Director of Indexing Services for the H. W. Wilson Company and the current editor of *Sears List of Subject Headings.* He is the seventh person since Minnie Earl Sears to edit *Sears List* since it began in 1923 under the title *List of Subject Headings for Small Libraries.* Joseph earned a master's degree in library and information science from Brigham Young University. Following graduation, he was hired by the H. W. Wilson Company, where he has worked ever since.

Gregory R. New wrote "Sources for Dewey Numbers" while serving as Assistant Editor of the Dewey Decimal Classification toward the end of a long career at the Library of Congress. Apart from two years in the Army (1951–53) and a year earning a library degree at Emory University (1954), he worked at the Library from 1948 to 2004. He was a Dewey classifier in the Decimal Classification Division from 1968 until he became Assistant Editor in 1985. His most noted achievements were a complete revision of the Dewey public administration schedule (350–354) and a quite extensive revision of the life sciences schedule (570–590).

[Note: The following was written about Gregory by a longtime Library colleague and friend.] Gregory recently retired from the Decimal Classification Division of LC after working at the Library for fifty years! He was the liaison to the Cataloging of Children's Materials Committee for longer than any of us remember, and we miss him.

Pamela J. Newberg is Manager of the Cataloging Department at Follett Library Resources in McHenry, Illinois, where she supervises a team of catalogers, cataloging paraprofessionals, and annotation writers. The group is responsible for cataloging nearly 1,500 books and video and audio materials each week. Pam holds a trio of higher education degrees, including a master of library science degree from Dominican University, a master of music degree from DePaul University, and a master of arts in teaching degree from National-Louis University. Pam brings a unique array of qualifications to her task as coauthor, having worked as a cataloger, children's librarian, and automation librarian in a number of settings, including school, public, academic, and special libraries. She is also an instructor at the College of Lake County (Illinois) in the Library Technical Assistant program. In addition to her academic and professional pursuits, Pam volunteers as a foster mother to abandoned kittens. She lives in Buffalo Grove, Illinois, with her teenage son and four cats.

Virginia M. Overberg is Manager, Book Cataloging, for Baker and Taylor Inc. in Bridgewater, New Jersey, a position she has held since 2000. She joined the company in 1987 as a cataloger and was promoted to Senior Cataloger in 1990, serving in that capacity as department trainer and cataloging policy manager. She has been cataloging since 1979, having gotten her start in academic libraries before joining the vendor cataloging world. Virginia has served on the Association for Library Collections and Technical Services Cataloging and Classification Section (ALCTS/CCS) Cataloging of Children's Materials Committee as both a past member and liaison. She is a representative to the Cataloging in Publication Advisory Group and the MicroLIF Community. In addition, she is a member of the Rutgers University Alumni Career Network and participates as a mentor in the ALCTS/CCS Education, Training, and Recruitment for Cataloging Committee's mentoring program.

Judith Yurczyk is a Resource Specialist at Follett Software Company. She is currently responsible for overseeing the content of the WebPath Express and State Standards products as well as serving as the MARC resource for the company. She writes "Tag of the Month," which features a new topic every month, accessible on Follett Software's home page, and responds to the "Ask MsMARC" inquiries. Judith is the author of Follett's *MARC Bibliographic Guide* and *MARC Authority Format Guide*. In addition, she has taught MARC workshops around the country. Judith received her MLS from the University of Wisconsin, Milwaukee. She is a member of the American Library Association (ALA), the Association for Library Collections and Technical Services (ALCTS) and its Cataloging and Classification Section (ALCTS/CCS), and Online Audiovisual Catalogers (OLAC), and has served as a member of the ALCTS/CCS Cataloging of Children's Materials Committee and the Vendor Relations Committee.

Index